RISE ABOVE

Overcoming the challenges of small business

NICOLA WARD

Published in Australia by Colbeggie Group Pty Ltd

First published in Australia 2024

This edition published 2024

Copyright © Nicola Ward 2024

Cover design, typesetting: WorkingType (www.workingtype.com.au)

ISBN: 978-0-646-89159-0

About the Author

Nicola Ward holds a Diploma in Office Management and a Certificate in Executive and Organisational Coaching. She is a registered BAS Agent, and an Everything Disc Practitioner.

Her life story has evolved from various roles in small business operations to now being a savvy and successful small business owner.

With over 25 years in business management and bookkeeping, Nicola collaborates with established and start up business owners to help grow their businesses, offering practical and down-to-earth advice and guidance.

In *Rise Above*, Nicola has included real-life advice from other business owners who have navigated the ups and downs of their business worlds.

Nicola's end goal was that her book would provide an engaging, candid and compelling read for all start up and established small business owners – job done!

Acknowledgements

I want to give a big shout-out to my family and friends for putting up with me during the whole writing process. Your support means everything, and I couldn't have done it without you.

A heartfelt thank you to my amazing clients, both past and present, for inspiring this book. Your input has been invaluable, and your stories have made these pages richer.

To everyone who played a role in bringing this project to life—thank you. Your contributions, big and small, have made a real difference.

Much love,
Nicola

Contents

In the Beginning

Do you have a great product idea? Are you providing a service? Or do you just want to be your own boss and start a business? You may think: Surely it's not that hard, doing what you love and making money at the same time.

Yet, starting a business is not as easy as it sounds, and there are many challenges, mistakes and frustrations on your journey to becoming successful.

Having worked with an array of small businesses over the last 26 years, one of the warning signs that I see from those in the early stages of starting a business is that they are not fully prepared for what lies ahead. Often this is not entirely their fault: You don't know what you don't know! Right?

There is also the misconception that you can 'live the dream' of entrepreneur, kick back, and others will take care of the work... but starting a business takes up a lot of time, money, sweat and tears, not to mention a great deal of sacrifice; and, of course, the many lessons learnt along the way until you get things right.

The Australian Bureau of Statistics (ABS) defines small businesses as those with less than 20 employees. Over 97% of all Australian businesses were small businesses in June 2022. Micro Business are those that have 1-4 employees. This also includes sole traders with no employees [1]

Will you see the warning signs? Small businesses, by their very nature, face unique challenges and uncertainties.

In the early years of my career, I worked closely with small businesses, and I witnessed firsthand the common mistakes that can occur. Alongside this, as Office Manager or Senior Bookkeeper, i.e., a managerial position, I felt responsible for some of these challenges. From financial blunders to operational hiccups, these situations were not only challenging from a professional standpoint, but they also took a toll emotionally, causing me to feel embarrassed and unsure. At times, when I was directly involved, some problems had me doubting my abilities. When challenges were not involving me directly, I didn't find it difficult to speak up. I am known to be honest and upfront and will say it how it is, but I found it's often harder when your respect is on the line.

Instead of dwelling on these regular small business frustrations, I chose to view them as stepping stones for improvement. Each of these served as a valuable lesson,

---

1   (Australian Small Business and Family Enterprise Ombudsman n.d.)

teaching me to approach problematic situations with caution, conduct thorough analysis, and seek input from others when needed. By learning from these experiences, I refined my problem-solving skills and developed a keen sense of foresight to prevent similar issues in the future.

Such problem-solving skills can benefit not only small business owners but anyone facing challenges in their professional or personal lives. By adopting a problem-solving mindset, you can approach obstacles calmly and proactively. Instead of becoming overwhelmed or discouraged by setbacks, you can view them as opportunities for growth and improvement.

These encounters and setbacks enabled me to cultivate resilience and adaptability. Small businesses often operate in rapidly changing environments, where the ability to quickly pivot and learn from errors is crucial for survival and growth. Embracing these challenges head on, I became adept at identifying areas for improvement and implementing effective solutions. If I had refused to take responsibility and allowed myself to have a fragile ego, this negative mindset would have prevented the growth of resilience and adaptability needed to thrive in the ever-changing world of small business.

Working in different departments of small businesses has taught me how everything and everyone are connected.

I've realised that working together and communicating effectively is crucial for avoiding mistakes. When we encourage learning and growth as a team, we can prevent errors and make the business stronger and more able to handle difficulties.

Reflecting on these experiences, I recognise that mistakes, challenges and frustrations (though initially daunting) are invaluable teachings. They serve as reminders that growth and progress often emerge from moments of adversity. By embracing the lessons learnt, I have been able to refine my skills, develop a deeper understanding of small business operations, and become a more effective professional.

Jumping in With Two Feet

Moving on from being an employee, I decided it was time to leave the security of employment and become a contract Bookkeeper. It was during this time that I became even more involved with new small business owners. I was fortunate enough to work with clients who allowed me to dive headfirst into the nitty-gritty of business set up and I found myself soaking up information like a sponge, eagerly absorbing everything I could about starting and running a business.

In a general contractor role, I got the chance to assist with the logistical set up of a building. It was a whirlwind, juggling the

responsibilities of dealing with local council and the various permits that are involved, contractors coming in to renovate, employing staff, managing rosters, buying equipment, taking bookings, organising events, helping out at events, and job costings; I even did some quoting of construction jobs under the watchful eye of an estimator. And, of course, the very important financial side of the business was always at the core of my work. I witnessed firsthand the triumphs and challenges of running a business from the ground up.

While working as a contract Bookkeeper, my curiosity led me to investigate other areas of business. I completed a Certificate in Executive and Organisational Coaching and became a Member of the International Coaching

Federation. This marked the beginning of my coaching journey assisting individuals who were wanting to start a business, along with helping established business owners in time management and goal setting. During this time, I completed some Leadership Coaching with one of my clients, becoming their cultural leader, and was heavily involved when it came to interviewing and retaining staff.

My interest in organisational culture grew, which prompted me to become a Certified Everything Disc Practitioner. 'Everything DISC' is an assessment tool that helps people better understand themselves and others and it has become a significant part of my expertise. I have performed over 250 'Everything DISC' profiles and delivered 12 workshops for groups over different industries.

This extensive knowledge across different aspects of a business gave me the foundations to start my own business.

After 12 years of working for others in Australia, Precious Time Business Services was born. I take great pride in the accomplishments I have made over the past three years, despite encountering various challenges along the way.

Precious Time Business Services has certainly had its fair share of ups and downs. There is one stand-out mistake that I made early on at the beginning of Precious Time, and it's a story I share with all potential clients, in the hope that they will then take the valuable lesson I learnt and apply it to their own business, and perhaps pass it on to other budding entrepreneurs. You can read all about my mistake and the very valuable lesson that I took from it in the chapter, 'Stick to What You're Good At'.

Having a small business can often feel like a lonely place to be, but luckily there is lots of support out there. Whether it be a business networking group, friends who are in business, government-funded initiatives, or even reading tips on mental health and wellbeing (an area which is so important when you have your own small business), there is something for everyone.

This book draws inspiration from my personal experiences and connections with numerous clients and vendors, particularly working closely with small businesses. The upcoming chapters don't aim to provide a comprehensive instructional guide, but rather serve as a practical road map. Having navigated the complexities of different industries and witnessed the unique challenges faced by these businesses, I want to share this knowledge.

Both down to earth and actionable, Rise Above reflects the kind of guidance I typically offer people already in business who require some help, or people who are navigating through the early stages of their business. I've included valuable insights from clients, sharing their accounts of mistakes, challenges, lessons, and motivations, providing you with a shortcut on your journey to success.

The Small Business failure rate in Australia is 33% in the first year, while just over 50% make it past four years.[2]

---

2 (Australian Small Business and Family Enterprise Ombudsman n.d.)

CHAPTER 1
HIGHLIGHTS

☑ **Business Planning**

☑ **SWOT Analysis**

☑ **Sales and Marketing Planning**

CHAPTER 1
Crafting your Road Map

Starting and running a small business can be a tough and sometimes scary journey. The key to success or failure often comes down to one vital point: planning well. Without a strong plan, the road ahead can be risky, with the possibility of dreams being crushed and money troubles piling up. In the competitive and ever-changing business world, those who don't plan risk ending up being among the unsuccessful. But don't worry because planning will help you to navigate these challenging circumstances and achieve success.

The Importance of Planning

Planning is the key to success for any small business. It acts as a road map, helping you wisely manage resources, set clear goals, and make informed decisions. By planning ahead, your business can stay ahead of the competition by anticipating challenges, spotting opportunities, and adapting to changes.

Planning cash flows also promotes financial stability, as it allows you to create realistic budgets, forecast income and expenses, and secure any necessary funding. Additionally, it facilitates effective resource management by outlining staffing needs, technology requirements, and operational processes.

Ultimately, planning empowers you to align your activities with the long-term vision of creating a strong foundation for sustainable growth.

The Starting Point

The journey of creating your own business cannot be compared to a 9-5 employee. It's a big step to change perspective from being an employee to becoming a business owner. The first step is taking time to explore yourself by assessing your own strengths and weaknesses. This will help you to make informed decisions and avoid potential mistakes. One way of assessing this is by doing a SWOT analysis.

What is a SWOT?

SWOT is a tool used to assess the strengths, weaknesses, opportunities and threats of your business.

Strengths – What do you do well? What unique resources can you draw on? What do others see as your strengths?

Weaknesses – What could you improve? Where do you have fewer resources than others? What are others likely to see as weaknesses?

Opportunities – What opportunities are open to you? What trends could you take advantage of? How can you turn your strengths into opportunities?

Threats – What threats could harm you? What is your competition doing? What threats do your weaknesses expose you to?

Why do a SWOT Analysis?

A SWOT analysis is similar to a road map, as it identifies important factors to be aware of and highlights key areas that require immediate attention and consideration.

Conducting a SWOT analysis allows you to gain insight into the different areas of your business that require improvement and find out where you can leverage existing opportunities to your advantage.

A thorough SWOT analysis should also shed light on potential obstacles and provide guidance on when and how to address them effectively.

"Understanding all areas of running a business and understanding what my weak areas were would have been one of my biggest challenges" – Sophie Budd, past Owner of Taste Budds Cooking Studio.

Had Sophie used the SWOT analysis tool, it would have helped her identify her strengths and weaknesses and assisted with making better decisions.

Free SWOT Analysis Tool

Business SWOT
Take Stock of Your Business

PART 1: Initial Assessment

INSTRUCTIONS: Think about the direction you would like your business to head in and answer the questions below.

NOTE: The more honestly and openly you answer the questions, the more helpful it will be.

	POSITIVE	NEGATIVE
INTERNAL	**STRENGTHS** What do you do well? What do you better than others? What unique strengths and talents do you have? What do others see as your strengths? What are you proud of or really like about your business?	**WEAKNESSES** What could you do better? What do you avoid? Where are others doing better than you? What are others likely to see as weaknesses? What do you need to face up to?
EXTERNAL	**OPPORTUNITIES** What opportunities are out there for you? What trends could you take advantage of? Which strengths could you turn into opportunities? What is going on locally that you could capitalise on?	**THREATS** What trends and threats could harm you? What is your competition doing? What threats do your weaknesses expose you to? What obstacles do you have coming up?

The Next Phase

A Business Plan is more than just a document; it's the backbone of a small business. It is a carefully crafted road map that turns your dreams into reality. By outlining your objectives, target audience, marketing strategies, financial projections, and operations, a business plan acts as a compass, guiding the business towards sustainable growth and profitability. It also communicates the essence of the business to investors, partners, employees, and customers. Additionally, it forces you to analyse ideas, identify risks, and develop contingency plans, enabling informed decision making and adaptability. With a well-structured business plan, you can navigate uncertainties, attract funding, and maximise your chances of long-term success.

There are many versions of a business plan, ranging from plans that are quite lengthy and complex to plans that comprise only one page and are quite simple and straightforward.

Although simple, a one-page business plan is better than not having one at all. The one- page business plan looks at:

1. *Value proposition – If you are at a party and someone asks what your business does, would you be able to describe it in one sentence?*

2. *Market need –The functional needs, desires and goals of your customer and the problems you solve for your customer.*

3. *Your solution – Can you describe your product or service and why it is better than the alternatives in the marketplace?*

4. *Target market – Describe your ideal customer. Who are they?*

5. *Competition – Who will your customer buy from if they are not going to buy from you?*

6. *Sales channels – These are the places where you will sell your products.*

7. *Marketing activities – What will you do to market your business and how many leads and customers will you need?*

8. *Budget and sales goals – How much will it cost to run your business? What sales targets do you need to reach to make the business successful?*

9. *Milestones – What are the major goals you need to accomplish to get the business up and running?*

10. Team – If the team is just you, write a couple of points on why you are the right person to run the business.

Justin Hillier said, "Planning is a very important stage of running a business. No matter what you're planning for, whether it's budgets, forecasts, workforce, strategies etc., always ensure you have a contingency plan for your contingency plan, because you will find that your first few may not succeed" - Justin Hillier from JCK Recruitment

Building the Blueprint

Maintaining a business plan is essential for addressing predicaments, rather than simply just storing it away in SharePoint and forgetting about it. Your plan should be updated and aligned with the business's current situation to remain relevant in the evolving business landscape. Updating your business plan becomes especially critical when significant changes take place, enabling you to effectively adapt and accommodate the shift. Even if there are no real changes, you should review your business plan annually.

By updating your business plan, you are essentially establishing new objectives to strive for. Additionally, documenting your revised business strategy ensures its availability for sharing with potential business partners, investors, and employees.

Sharing your business plan with employees has its benefits. It promotes transparency and helps everyone understand the goals and direction. When employees align their goals with the business vision, they collaborate better and propel the business forward.

FREE One page Business Plan   EXAMPLE

ONE PAGE BUSINESS PLAN TEMPLATE

EXAMPLE:

IDENTITY	
We offer high-quality biking gear for families and ever day people not just gear heads	

PROBLEM WORTH SOLVING	OUR SOLUTION
Its not easy to buy a new bike in this town without knowing a cycling expert	• New Bike • Repairs • University Patrol • Clothing and Accessories • Used Bikes

TARGET MARKET	COMPETITION
• College students • Young families • Trail enthusiasts • Parents	• Local bike shops • Big Retailers • Online stores

SALES CHANNELS	MARKETING ACTIVITIES
We sell bikes and accessories directly to customers through our bike shop. We also sell via our online store and at special bike events.	• Host social media pages and website • Partner with local Tourist Board • Attend outdoor enthusiast trade shows • Grand Opening with deals

REVENUE	EXPENSES
• New Bikes • Repairs • University Patrol • Clothing	• Inventory • Payroll • Marketing

MILESTONES				
Milestone 1 01/01/2024	Milestone 2 01/03/2024	Milestone 3 31/03/2024	Milestone 4 30/06/2024	Milestone 5 31/12/2024

TEAM & KEY ROLES	PARTNERS & RESOURCES
• **Joe Bloggs (Founder)** • **Jess Smith (Store Manager)**	• **Australian Cycle Tours** • **Bikes Parts "R" Us** • **The Great Outdoors**

Sales and Marketing Plan

Many business owners also have a marketing plan separate from their business plan, which goes into more detail on how the goals can be achieved. While the business plan shapes everything about the way your business will work and lays out the bigger goals and ideas, the marketing plan focuses more on making your potential customer aware and likely to buy your product or service.

Rachel Huber from Bare Digital has worked with numerous new business owners, including myself, and she said, "Typically, most prospective/new business owners undervalue the time and resources needed for marketing and sales to generate a consistent pipeline of customers. They formulate marketing plans based on assumptions ('everyone I talked to thinks it's a great idea') rather than current data."

Rachel suggests, "Before investing in anything for your business, conduct thorough market research relating to current market conditions:

1. *Level of demand – Using keyword research tools, look at the search volume in your region for related keywords for the last 3 months.*

2. *Market saturation – Do a Google and social search for similar terms and see how many competitors pop up.*

3. *Prospective market size.*

4. *Economic indicators - Can your target market afford to buy it right now?*

5. *Pricing"*

Here are Rachel's tips:

Develop a sales and marketing plan taking these factors into account. Most people think building a website and launching social media accounts ticks all the boxes for marketing. Worldwide, over 250,000 new websites are launched daily. Over 310 million businesses have social media profiles.

- How do you compete with the millions of other businesses for traffic?

  - Are you willing to pay for it? i.e. Search or social ads, SEO campaigns, etc.

- If paid, can you support campaigns for 6+ months? Engagement can take time to build.

- How much time will you invest in developing your marketing assets?

  - How often will you post new content?

  - Do you have the resources to generate and post new content? i.e. support staff, equipment, photography skills, video editing software, etc.

- Are you diversifying your marketing channels?

  - Which channels will reach your target demographics?

  - Which channels suit the stages of your customer journey? i.e. social and search for the exposure stage; email marketing for those in the consideration stage.

  - How will you store prospect/customer data securely and safely?

- What's your allocation of labour, and who's responsible for every task?

- Do you have these tasks accounted for in your daily time management?

- How much time and ad spend are your competitors investing?

  - What marketing channels are they using?

  - Do they have dedicated sales personnel?

"Your customer acquisition needs to be a primary focus for your time and resources, with marketing and sales tactics built on data and research, rather than assumptions, to be successful"
– Rachel Huber from Bare Digital

By integrating these planning elements, you can create a cohesive road map for success. You can leverage insights from SWOT analysis, incorporate it into the business plan, and align marketing strategies accordingly. Reviewing what happens is also important. Understanding the challenges and mistakes that arise from inadequate planning allows you to take practical measures, setting your venture on a path towards growth and prosperity.

Remember, planning is an ongoing process that requires continuous evaluation and adjustment, so you should embrace flexibility and a learning mindset to adapt to changing market dynamics.

CHAPTER 2
HIGHLIGHTS

☑ **Mission Statement**

☑ **Business Values**

☑ **Vision**

CHAPTER 2
North Star

Running a small business can be a rollercoaster ride, filled with highs and lows. It's easy to get lost in the day-to-day tasks and lose sight of the bigger picture. That's where your North Star comes in. It serves as your guiding light, giving you direction and motivation when faced with challenges.

Understanding your 'why' is incredibly important. It forms the foundation of your business's mission, vision, and values. It defines the problem you're solving and the impact you want to make in the world. Your 'why not' only drives you forward but may also resonate with your customers, employees, and stakeholders, creating a sense of purpose and unity.

The Why

"When we know WHY we do what we do, everything falls into place. When we don't, we have to push things into place"
—Simon Sinek

How often do we ask ourselves: Why does my business exist?

Seems like a straightforward and simple question, but people do find it hard to answer. Nevertheless, when you are able to answer, it will give you a clear purpose of why your business should exist. Your 'why' is also known as a mission statement.

Some owners can find themselves caught up with the day-to-day operations, which can often lead to forgetting about important business strategies.

Aldo Sal Margio, Director of Cyclus & Bicep Labour, said one of the most valuable lessons he learnt early in business was about keeping in mind the vision and plan.

"Being a young business owner can be an exhilarating and daring experience, but it's easy to become consumed with day-to-day operations and overlook important aspects of the business. Unfortunately, my business partner and I fell into this trap and spent years

in a vicious cycle of working in the business rather than on it. As a result, our company didn't achieve the level of success we had anticipated after four years in operation.

Despite our busyness, exhaustion, extensive development, and rapid growth, our business still wasn't profitable. It wasn't until we took the time to focus on the bigger picture and work on the business that we began to identify where we were falling short and what we had been neglecting."

When being faced with this same problem in your own business, going back and revisiting your 'why' and your clear vision for the future can help identify the bigger picture.

Here are some tips on how to draft your 'why' (or vision).

Define your business's purpose

Describe what your business aims to accomplish. You probably noted this down while creating your business plan, so you can draw from there. You have the best understanding of the business, so write down in a clear and concise manner what your small business intends to achieve.

Define the values behind how your business achieves its goals

Although you may love to discuss the 'how' of your operations, your customers don't necessarily need to know the intricate details of your service's production process. Instead, they want to understand your values and how they contribute to achieving your objectives in an exceptional way.

Define why your business does what it does

This is where it becomes exciting. Grab a cup of coffee, play some music, and tap into the passion behind your business. This element of your mission statement will inspire customers to invest their money and loyalty in your product. Think about why you want to start or why you started your business. What emotions did you experience that motivated you to endure the challenges of starting a business? Many people have ideas but only a few take action. What motivated you to act on yours?

Revise, edit, repeat

Aim to refine your work by engaging in the process of editing and revising. A well-crafted mission statement should be concise and memorable, capable of serving as a powerful motto for your business. You should be able to effortlessly incorporate it, or its variations, into your marketing campaigns, social media platforms, and overall product delivery.

This final result will become your valuable tool for effectively communicating with customers, local businesses, and the wider community.

Therefore, don't shy away from making lots of edits. Get input from close friends, family members, and teammates to hear how it actually sounds and if it resonates with them.

When Mike McCracken was asked: "What are some of the biggest challenges you have faced in your business so far?" included in his answer was; "Lack of direction or a clear path of where I wanted to take the business or why I am even in business." Michael McCracken, Director of Boss Carpentry WA, originally Express Fixing, founded in 2005

Continually working and updating your 'why' as the business grows and moves will help answer the question: Why am I even in business? The lines can often become blurred as you face the many challenges that arise as a small business owner.

So, if the purpose addresses the 'why', let's have a look at the 'how'.

Values

Small businesses are characterised by their unique values. The values define the culture and become a guiding light for the business.

What are Values?

Values are the core principles, beliefs, and guiding philosophies that shape the culture and behaviour of business. Well-chosen values help support your purpose.

An example of using your values with clients comes from Luke Hall.

> *"Probably my biggest mistakes related to not following my instincts. If you feel like someone's unlikely to pay you or is going to be a difficult client, then you're probably right. Having an appropriate screening process in place so you only work with people who reflect your values is important, and reduces the likelihood of becoming involved in disputes with difficult counterparties."*
> – Luke Hall, Director, Eaton Hall Corporate & Commercial Lawyers

Values are not just words; they serve as the very foundation for your operations; they shape the relationships with your customers, employees, and the community. Your business values form the core principles that guide your decisions and actions. By adhering to these values, you establish your business identity, build strong relationships, and create a positive impact.

Ultimately, your small business values contribute to your success.

Values vary from one business to another, even when in the same competitive space, as they originate from the owners of the business. So embrace your authenticity and let your values reflect your true essence. Select values that not only stand out but also hold significance. Choose values that truly represent the desired behaviour for your employees and yourself, rather than adopting them just because they seem trendy, feel nice, or everyone else is using them.

If your business hasn't established a set of values yet, here's a simple process to help you identify and develop them:

1. Start by considering your own personal principles and beliefs and how they relate to the values you want for your business.

Ask yourself:

What do I value in other businesses as both an employee and a customer?

What values are essential to my business?

2. Gather a group of people who can collaborate to develop the values for your business.

If your business is new and doesn't have staff yet, seek trusted individuals from outside the business to assist you, such as mentors, friends, or business advisors.

If your business is already operating with staff, choose people who understand the company culture, display leadership skills, and are key to the business's functioning. This may be the leadership team or your senior staff.

3. Identify the categories of values that are most relevant to your business.

Challenge your team or your group of friends, business advisors or mentors to create your impact values – these are values that outline the positive impact the business can have on other people and the environment.

4. Draft your values. Keep them concise and straightforward, using 1 to 2 words or a short phrase. You might need to provide a brief explanation of the meaning of the values but avoid making the values overly complicated. Clear and concise values are easier for employees to remember and for customers and stakeholders to embrace.

Values in Practice

Two of my clients have values that are not generic. Their values have then been made into posters, to stand out, and for employees, suppliers and clients to see.

SMS Group Services

Be reliable, be there when needed.

Find better ways, don't be scared of change.

BE RELIABLE, BE THERE WHEN NEEDED

OUR MEANING

At SMS when the job needs to be done it needs to be done. This could be finishing a task at the end of the day for a fresh start in the morning. It could be a breakdown at one of our sites which requires urgent action. It could be getting the invoicing finished for the end of the period. It could be recruiting six people at the drop of a hat.

At SMS our reliability defines us to our clients and guarantees ongoing work.

FIND BETTER WAYS DON'T BE SCARED OF CHANGE

OUR MEANING

The only constant in this world is change.

Since 2001, SMS has adapted and evolved to the needs of the everchanging market to grow and thrive.

Don't be a dinosaur but remember the crocodile.

SafeStyle Pty Ltd

Harmony – Meaning: Open Communication, Epic Culture, Everyone in Sync, Inclusive and diverse, from the worksite to the weekend.

Adventurous – Meaning: Pushing boundaries, being out of your comfort zone, determination and ambition, breaking the mould.

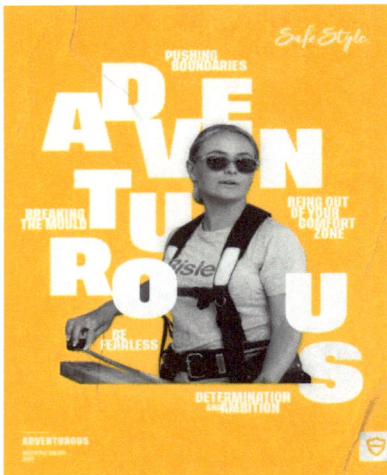

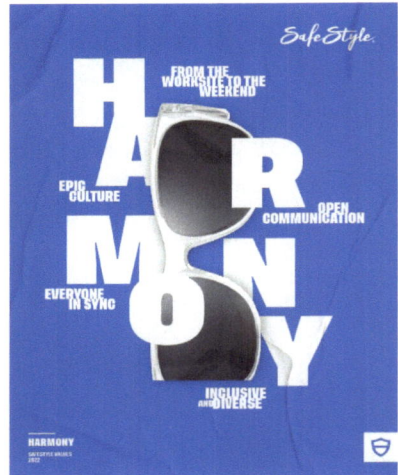

Implementing your Business Values

Defining and communicating company culture and values can be challenging. To ensure everyone feels connected and engaged, consider the following:

Lead by example: All leaders should consistently demonstrate and embody the core values. This is also the case if you are a sole trader.

Incorporate values in hiring and onboarding: Make sure new hires understand and align with the company values from the start.

Emphasise values in all communication: Make core values a central part of your communication strategy.

Recognise employee contributions: Clearly demonstrate that recognising and appreciating employees' efforts is an important company value, motivating them to go the extra mile. One idea is you could do a value embodiment award each month, or quarter.

Once you have values and you have embedded them, you cannot just set and forget them; the execution of the values is critical. No matter how great your company values sound, first of all, live by them: lead by example, put them before profit, and never compromise.

Aldo stayed true to his values and focus, as reflected in the biggest challenges he has faced in business so far.

"Saying NO! Shiny new toys and time-consuming projects can be detrimental to a business's success. Our lack of business experience and clients' demands for our involvement led to us saying 'yes' to everything, causing stress and hindering productivity.

As we became more successful and gained control over our operations, we still found ourselves reverting to old habits and saying 'yes' to jobs and projects we didn't need to take on. Learning to say 'no' has had a significant impact on our happiness, mental health, productivity, leadership, and involvement as directors.

As I once said, 'It is impossible to steer a ship away from danger and into the sun when you are face down scrubbing the deck.'"

Saying 'no' can be difficult, but it is crucial to the success of a business. It allows for better time management, improved mental health, and a focus on projects that truly benefit the company."

Vision

Defining your vision provides you with a clear direction and long-term perspective on what your business aims to achieve. It serves as a guiding principle that shapes your business's goals, strategy, and culture. Your vision statement provides direction, purpose and inspiration for you and your employees.

When creating your vision, consider the following:

Ask yourself:

- What is your purpose?

- What are your goals?

- What are your values?

- What sort of culture do you want?

- Where do you see yourself in 1 year, 5 years and 10 years?

- Have your key staff and or friends help you brainstorm ideas.

Creating a vision statement

Your vision statement should be clear and concise, be future oriented, inspiring and motivating, and ambitious but also realistic. It should serve as a guiding light and align the actions and decisions of everyone involved in your business.

As your business grows, your purpose and vision will change. That's why you should revisit them every couple of years to ensure they are current and help you deliver on your goals. Your values should remain constant, but keep in mind that may require a little tweaking as the business grows.

When Tim Lewis, Founder of SafeStyle Pty Ltd, was asked "What are some of the biggest challenges you've faced in your business so far? How did you overcome them?" He answered,

"My biggest challenge was learning how an actual business operates efficiently. I originally worked for a small plumbing company that was very laid back. I had never managed a team or been responsible for multiple staff, so this all came incredibly fast. I pushed through and learnt the basics, outsourced the marketing and the fulfilment of daily orders to hopefully free up my time to learn the next steps. But once I made a few changes there, the orders went up, which meant customer service went up, the stress of ordering more stock went up, the demand for new products went up, and so forth... So instead of looking for staff and learning how to set up an efficient team to delegate to, I decided to just put my head down and work even harder to stay on top of the workload. I didn't have another option, as I just didn't have the experience, skills or understanding on where to even start to build a team... I suppose the thought of it was just too overwhelming for me. After two years, I burnt out; I realised I needed to get help, fast!

So, I finally put my hand up and I was lucky enough to be surrounded by amazing people that helped show me the ropes, and from the hard work in the previous years I was able to hire a best friend of mine. Lewis came onboard and helped set up some foundations to start building the team and we started learning rapidly from mentors who quickly turned into best friends and full time SafeStyle employees. But that year of onboarding staff at a rapid rate was the most stressful time of my *career, as I was so far out of my comfort zone in so many ways. But once I put my hand out for help and learnt to let go and delegate, it all took a turn for the better. From the help of most of the current team here at SafeStyle today, we worked hard together with full team training sessions to align our mission, vision and values and hire the right people to keep growing to reach our goals.*

I realised the best boss is someone who employs more experienced and skilled people than themselves. The best boss should be motivating and lead the team forward with ambitious goals."

Your North Star serves as a constant reminder of why your business exists, its core values, and long-term goals. They help you stay focused, make smart decisions, and adapt to changes while staying true to yourself and your business's essence. These principles, the 'why', values, and vision statement all drive your business forward on its journey towards sustainable growth, meaningful impact, and continued success.

🎈 **Mission, Vision & Value Tool**

CHAPTER 3
HIGHLIGHTS

☑ **Business Structures**

☑ **Business Registrations**

☑ **Regulatory Compliance**

☑ **Terms and Conditions**

☑ **Legal Responsibilities When Employing Staff**

CHAPTER 3
Navigating the
Compliance Maze

Compliance is a vital aspect of starting and running a successful small business in Australia. From legal regulations and industry standards to financial obligations and ethical considerations, ensuring compliance in all areas can be a challenging task. However, it is essential for you to understand and meet these requirements in order to operate legally and ethically, and to minimise risks.

Compliance should not be viewed as an onerous obligation, but rather as an opportunity for growth and long-term success. By embracing a proactive and strategic approach to compliance, you can establish trust with stakeholders, enhance operational efficiency, and protect your reputation in an increasingly competitive market.

So where do you start?

Start at the Beginning

When starting a business, it's crucial to select the right structure that fits your requirements at the time. However, as your business grows you might change your structure. The main options for business structures are sole trader, partnership, trust, and company.

What is a Sole Trader?

A sole trader is an individual who operates a business. This structure is considered the most straightforward and cost-effective approach.

By operating as a sole trader, you are:

- the sole proprietor and manager of your business.

- legally accountable for all aspects of the business, including any debts or losses incurred in its operation.

While you can hire employees for your business, you cannot employ yourself.

What is a Partnership?

A partnership is when a group of individuals come together to operate a business and divide the profits or losses among all the partners.

While a written agreement is not legally necessary, it can be highly beneficial to have one in place to prevent misunderstandings and conflicts regarding each partner's contributions, to specify how income and losses will be shared, and to outline the management of the business. Without a written agreement, the partners typically split the income and losses equally.

It's important to note that partners in a partnership are not considered employees of the partnership, but they do have the ability to hire other workers.

What is a Trust?

If a trust is created to run a business, there will be a document called a Trust Deed that explains what the trustees can do and how the people who benefit from the trust are involved.

The trustee is in charge of handling the trust's taxes. The trustee can be one person or a company. Normally, the money the trust makes each year is shared among the people who benefit from it. They are called beneficiaries.

What is a Company?

A company is like a separate entity in the eyes of the law.

It has its own responsibilities for taxes and employee retirement funds. The company's money and everything it owns belong to the company, not the people who own shares in it. If you use the company's money or any of its belongings for personal reasons, there may well be tax consequences.

The company can share its profits with the shareholders by giving them dividends. Sometimes, the company can also give the shareholders credits for the taxes it has already paid on its profits.

While a company can protect its assets, the people who run the company, called directors, can still be held responsible for what they do. In some cases, they may be responsible for certain tax and superannuation fund debts of the company.

All directors of a company need to prove who they are, and obtain a special number, called a director ID, before they can become directors. Companies are watched over by a government organisation called ASIC.

Setting up and managing a company costs more than other types of business structures, and there are extra rules and the government imposes strict reporting rules that must be adhered to.

A lawyer and/or an accountant will be able to advise you on which is the correct structure for you and your needs at this point in time.

What registrations do you need?

Business name

Your business name is the name used for your business. It helps your customers recognise you and sets you apart from other businesses. Having a business name makes it easier for customers to feel connected to your business and brand.

So how do you register?

Before you register the name, you must check the availability of your chosen name. ASIC has a business name register which you can check to see if the name is available. There are other websites that you can use, but I would recommend using this one. ASIC provides an excellent step by step user guide to help you with the registration.

ASIC Step by Step Guide

You will also have to apply for an ABN (Australian Business Number) and, depending on which structure you choose, you may also need a TFN (Tax File Number) and an ACN (Australian Company Number).

If you are buying or selling goods and services, you may have to register for GST (Goods and Services Tax). If you think your turnover will reach the GST threshold (or more) in the first year of operation, you should register. The threshold amount is $75,000.00.

The ATO has an extensive guide on when and how to register for GST.

GST Registration

When you employ staff, you will also have to register for PAYG (Pay As You Go withholding tax). These are the amounts you withhold from employees as standard practice, or from businesses that do not quote their ABN. You must register with the ATO before you can withhold these amounts.

Pay as You Go Withholding Registration

Your Accountant and/or Lawyer can provide advice on which structure will suit your own personal situation. They can also help you with the registrations that you require, if it is not something that you want to tackle yourself.

Regulatory Compliance

Now that you have the business structure organised, you need to think about the licences and permits that you might need. Different industries have different licences and permits that are required to trade legally. These might include: building licence, heavy machinery licence, high risk work licence, food authority licence, liquor licence, responsible service of alcohol, Australian financial service licence, Working With Children Check, Police Check, and real estate agent licence, just to name a few.

There are a couple of websites you can use to check which licences and permits you will require for your particular industry and for which state/s you are trading in. Using these tools will give you peace of mind, knowing you will be compliant.

Licence and Permit Checker

As a BAS Agent and Certified Bookkeeper, for my business and for the running of my practice, I need to follow The Tax Agent Services Act 2009 (TASA), which is the legislation that applies to BAS agents in Australia. I am also a member of the Institute of Certified Bookkeepers.

Many of you will be professionals who charge for services who have professional standards and Acts that you need to follow, as well as being part of organisations where you are required to keep up relevant Continuing Professional Education (CPE) hours.

Trademarks

Do I need a trademark?
A trademark is like the face of your company. It's a special sign that makes your goods or services different from others. When customers see your trademark, they know where the products come from. A trademark also builds trust and shows that your goods or services are of good quality.

Think of it this way: terms like 'brand value', 'brand recognition', and 'brand recall' are closely connected to trademarks. The most successful brands in the world have unique trademarks that help consumers easily identify their products and believe that they are worth buying.

For example, brands like Nike, Target, Dominos, Ford and Google.

A trademark can be almost anything that sets your business apart, like a word, symbol, slogan, shape, sound, colour, or even a scent. It's like a special mark that you put on your goods or packaging to make them stand out and help consumers know they're from your company.

Choosing the right trademark is extremely important because it can bring many benefits. A good trademark helps your customers easily recognise you and remember the business, which can lead to long-term success.

On the other hand, selecting the wrong trademark can prove very costly. Not only will you waste money on developing and promoting a failed brand, but you could also face legal consequences if you neglect to check the database and infringe on another business's trademark or reputation. This could result in you having to pay damages. There is a free trademark checker available to use, which is a great tool and can keep you out of trouble!

Trademark Checker

Christine Tinley from Guides 4 Sight now knows how important this free checking tool is.

"I designed my own logo/trademark and corporate colours, focused on meeting the specific needs of people with low vision as this is my target market. I did a little bit of online searching under our business name & initials to see what else came up, but nothing triggered me as being comparable to my planned logo, so I went ahead and used it for three years or so before deciding to register it as a trademark with IP Australia. This was when another (multinational) company raised an objection to the proposed registration of my trademark. I then had to engage a Trademark Attorney to help me understand the process and negotiate with the other company as I was completely out of my depth. Luckily, our businesses are quite different, and thankfully it was all resolved practically and with a minimal fuss. However, it took two years of negotiating and higher than expected legal fees than if I had taken this path in the beginning, along with additional website and stationery costs. On a positive note: Many companies rebrand quite often – this is one rebrand for us in seven years and we now have a fresh new look that will last for quite a while."

Insurances

It's crucial to have insurance to protect you and your business, yet determining the right insurances for your business can be complex. Every business is unique, and factors such as your industry, trade, type of business, size, location, and if you employ staff or contractors, come into the equation. Different businesses face different challenges and risks, like a tradesperson compared to a real estate agent, coffee shop owner, or engineering firm. Even mobile or home-based hairdressers have different needs from salon owners with a physical shopfront.

Finding the right insurance is vital for managing the risks associated with running your business; an insurance broker can be of assistance in this area. Every business, regardless of size or industry, faces daily risks.

Some types of insurance may be mandatory for certain businesses due to legal requirements, professional board or association membership obligations, or contractual agreements with landlords or customers. Fortunately, there are now various combined insurance policy options available, and you can customise business insurance policies to meet your specific needs.

The main insurances that business owners should be considering are:

Public Liability – Protects you and your employees if your products or services cause harm or damage to someone else or their property.

Professional Indemnity – If you provide a service or advice, professional indemnity protects you against liability for damages, and the legal costs associated with defending yourself against claims arising from an act, omission, or breach of duty in the course of your work.

Workers Compensation - Under Australian law, employers must have workers compensation insurance to cover their workers in case they get sick or injured because of work. It is a safety net if your workers become injured or ill because of work.

There are several other types of insurances available, depending on the type of business you have and whether you have premises. Obtaining the services of a good broker should keep you on the right path, as they'll be able to advise on the insurances that you need as a minimum, and suggest other insurances you could take out that will keep you and your business safe and compliant.

Business Terms & Conditions

Why do I need these?

Having clear terms and conditions for your business helps reduce the misunderstandings between you and your customers and can help avoid disputes. It also saves you from spending a truck-load of money on legal battles.

The types of disputes you may encounter can be scope disputes, payment disputes and delivery disputes.

A business's terms and conditions are important and legally binding. For example, before customers buy something online, they usually need to agree to the supplier's terms and refund conditions, often by checking a box online.

A well-drafted agreement contains information such as:

- *the type of products provided*
- *delivery of the products*
- *payment terms*
- *protection of intellectual property and confidential information*
- *dispute resolution processes and termination*
- *Australian Consumer Law liabilities and disclaimers*

Engaging with a lawyer to provide you with this will ensure

that you have all the relevant areas of your business activities covered in the terms and conditions.

In my experience as a bookkeeper, there were times when clients have not had terms and conditions in place which presented huge challenges when dealing with disputes over the nonpayment of invoices. One client engaged the services of a debt collecting agency but soon discovered they could not help recover the money as no terms and conditions had been signed by the customer who owed my client money.

Needless to say, my client now has a new customer onboarding process where no work can be undertaken until the terms and conditions are signed by both parties. Since then, my client has used the services of the debt collecting agency and having those terms and conditions signed by the client has been crucial in the collection of the overdue invoice.

Legal Responsibilities when Employing Staff

It's a minefield!

Chapter 6 will delve into the details about your employees and the responsibilities you have as an employer. However, here is an overview of your obligations as a small business owner. It's crucial to either possess a solid understanding of these obligations or seek assistance from a qualified professional to navigate this complex landscape.

Here are some of the key obligations to consider:

Employment Responsibilities: You must comply with current laws which is usually by each State, including hiring practices, contracts, and working and pay conditions.

Taxation and Payroll: Managing payroll taxes, employee deductions, and submitting accurate reports to the ATO and other government agencies.

Health and Safety: Providing a safe work environment and adhering to safety regulations to protect your employees.

Benefits and Leave: Ensuring you have the appropriate benefits and leave policies, as required by law.

Discrimination and Harassment: Preventing discrimination and harassment in the workplace through policies and training.

Worker's Compensation: Ensuring you have adequate coverage to support employees in case of work-related injuries.

Employee Records: Maintaining accurate records of employee information and employment history.

Termination Procedures: Following legal procedures when terminating employees, including notice periods and severance pay when applicable.

Training and Development: Providing opportunities for employee growth and development to enhance their skills and productivity.

These are just a few of the many employer responsibilities you will encounter as a small business owner. A deeper understanding of each area is essential to maintain a successful and compliant business.

Navigating the compliance maze of small business can feel like a never-ending list of rules and regulations. Just when you think you've mastered it, a new rule or regulation appears, and keeping up with them all can feel like a full-time job. Remember, every twist and turn on your journey is a chance to learn and grow.

CHAPTER 4
HIGHLIGHTS

☑ **Multitasking and its Problems**

☑ **The Problems of Doing Too Much**

☑ **Strategies to Overcome Wearing Too Many Hats**

CHAPTER 4
Stick to What You Are Good At

In the fast-paced world of small businesses, you can often find yourself donning multiple hats to ensure the success of your venture. You are not just the boss; you are also the Accountant, the Marketing Manager, the Human Resources Manager, the Customer Service Manager, and many more. This juggling act might initially seem like a necessary and exhilarating part of the entrepreneurial journey, showcasing your adaptability and passion for your business. However, as time goes on, the burden of wearing too many hats can take its toll, both on the business and on your own wellbeing.

The Multitasking Challenge

Small business owners are no strangers to multitasking. It's not because we want to but because it's often necessary, due to limited resources. We might not have big teams or heaps of cash, so we have to do a bit of everything ourselves.

This can help us save money on expenses and stay closely involved with our business, but it's not all smooth sailing.

I am no stranger to the downfalls of wearing too many hats. When I first started Precious Time Business Services, I met with a marketing professional who came highly recommended, and they gave me a quote for a website. Although it was not overly expensive, I thought it was an expense, as a new small business owner, that I could do without. I didn't believe I needed a website anyway as most of my work comes from referrals. Asking around, many people I spoke with said that I should still have a website, even if it's just simple. So, not wanting to spend the money (the Scottish in me!) and with no experience, I set off to build a simple website. It can't be that hard, surely! It took me two full days (that's day and night) working away on it. I was happy with the result; it was basic and a bit rough to be honest, but it was done. I went to bed that night and could not sleep. All I could think about was the time that I had wasted doing a sub-par job. I had spent valuable time (billable time where I could have been charging my clients) compiling a substandard website. The very next day I emailed the company that had provided me with a quote for building and designing my website and told them to go ahead.

I am ever so glad that I never used my website, as the one I have now is fantastic. This was a great lesson for me. Now when something requires a professional service in my business that is not Bookkeeping or Coaching, I pay for someone else who is qualified to do this, leaving me to do what I do best.

The Problems of Doing Too Much

When you stretch yourself thin across different responsibilities, you risk encountering several challenges that can undermine the very success you seek to achieve. Below are some of the common problems you might encounter:

Not So Effective

When you're juggling a lot of tasks, it's hard to do each one really well. You might make mistakes, miss good opportunities, or waste time on things that don't matter much.

Burnout and Exhaustion

All this multitasking can lead to burnout and exhaustion. You may find yourself working long hours, sacrificing your personal life, and neglecting your health. This can have serious consequences not only for your wellbeing, but also for the sustainability of your business in the long run.

Bad Decision-Making: Multitasking can make your decision-making go haywire. When overwhelmed by the sheer volume of tasks and responsibilities, you may make hasty or ill-informed decisions that can negatively impact the business. Sound decision-making requires time and focus, which can be in short supply when wearing too many hats.

Missing Important Stuff

With so much on your plate, you could easily forget about some important parts of your business. For instance, you might focus so much on getting customers that you forget to keep an eye on your finances.

Impact on Product/Service Quality

The quality of your products or services can suffer when you're trying to do it all. You won't have enough time and energy to make things as good as they can be. That can lead to unhappy customers and a bad reputation.

Falling Behind the Competition

Keeping up with the competition is tough. If you're doing everything yourself, you might struggle against other businesses that have specialised teams or more resources for specific jobs like marketing or customer service.

James McCallister of The Good Creative knows only too well the implications of not sticking to what you're good at.

"Trying to be everything to everyone that shows an interest is a natural reaction, especially in the early days as you look to build a client base. Continually committing to short timelines and small budgets can certainly help to build a customer base, but you make a rod for your own back at the same time. People come to expect it all the time, it eventually wears thin, and you can end up resenting the client / customer for no real fault of their own. It's a fine line, especially when you need income, but not selling yourself short in the early days is a good lesson in hindsight. It's easier said than done."

Dr Ian Dunican of Melius Consulting recalls how wearing many hats was a mistake that he made in the first year of business:

"I attempted to handle my own invoicing despite not having the necessary expertise. There were a couple of reasons for this decision. Firstly, I believed that if I didn't do it myself, no one else would. While I had received business training, I had never worked as a bookkeeper or accountant. Although I understood the financial aspects and cost management, I quickly realised that invoicing was a daunting task. I concluded that it was best to leave it to professionals.

In looking ahead, there are two key aspects of my business that I will not compromise on. First and foremost is maintaining an effective website and handling media and communications. Secondly, I understand the importance of bookkeeping and financial services in my line of work. Without proper financial management, providing professional services becomes challenging, especially when it comes to invoicing clients. It's not a favourable look to have to chase clients for payment. Whilst wearing many hats may be seen as hustling, it can strain the client-provider relationship over time. This is where having a bookkeeper, who handles administrative tasks and follows up on dates diligently, makes a significant difference. It allows me to focus solely on delivering my services without being bogged down by financial concerns. I believe in the clear division of responsibilities. My role is to provide my expertise, not to get involved in the areas of the business that are not in my wheelhouse. My clients hire me to do the heavy lifting and solve problems for them."

Navigating Common Pitfalls

Ego and Control:

It's common for business owners to struggle with control. Overcome the ego-driven desire to do everything yourself by recognising that effective leadership involves collaboration.

Fear of Letting Go:

Fear often accompanies the thought of handing over responsibilities. Acknowledge this fear and gradually ease into delegation, starting with smaller tasks before moving on to more significant responsibilities.

Regular Self-Assessment:

Conduct regular self-assessments of your workload. Identify tasks that can be streamlined, automated, or delegated. Being aware of your responsibilities is the first step towards a more balanced workload.

Alex Toyne of Toyne & Associates regularly conducts self-assessments of his workload and said that a valuable lesson that he has learnt *was:*

"Wanting to only give positive responses to clients and subsequently overpromising when it comes to the amount of work that can be done in limited time frames, leading to high levels of stress and inevitably disappointing clients because you can't be in all places at once.

The lesson was to always manage expectations and give yourself enough time to do work properly. The client won't mind work taking a couple of extra days if that's what you've told them from the start, but if you promise something one week and don't get it to them until the following week then you'll be stressed, and they'll be disappointed."

Finding the Right Balance for Success

Recognising the drawbacks of wearing too many hats is essential. To help overcome these challenges and achieve sustainable growth, you need to find strategies that allow you to have a better balance in life. Below are some strategies that you can try.

Delegate

Get help! If you have capable people around you, share some of your tasks with them. Alternatively, you can hire experts for certain jobs or outsource tasks that aren't your strong suit. Sharing the load can improve your business and your life.

Stick to Your Strengths

Focus on what you're really good at. When you do what you excel in, you'll make a bigger impact on your business's success, as your passion and expertise not only drive innovation but also inspire confidence in your team and attract like-minded people, creating a harmonious force that propels your business to new heights.

Time Management

Be smart with your time. Prioritise tasks, set aside specific times for each job, and try not to switch between tasks too much. This keeps you focused, allows you to achieve more each day, and helps you avoid burnout.

Free Time Management Tools

Learn and Improve

If you need to do some jobs yourself, take the time to learn and get better at them. Education and training can make a big difference in how well you handle different roles.

Make Technology your friend!

Automation tools and software can make tasks easier and faster, like using an accounting software package; for example, Xero, MYOB or Reckon for handling your finances, or use the many software packages available for marketing. Embrace technology to save time and effort.

Seek Mentorship and Support

You could benefit from mentorship and support networks. You can often get subsidised programs and mentoring through your local Council. Connecting with other business owners who have faced similar challenges can provide valuable insights and guidance on how to navigate the complexities of small business.

Look After Yourself

Don't forget about self-care. Taking breaks, keeping a good work-life balance, and taking care of your physical and mental health are vital for long-term success.

Rachel Huber from Bare Digital knows only too well the challenges of not having that balance:

"The biggest challenge I've faced, and continue to face eight years on, is in work/life balance. In some aspects,

my work/life balance and mental state have improved drastically. While I work more hours than in previous corporate roles, I take breaks when it suits me. I've improved my fitness schedule and built my work hours around my workouts, so I'm in better shape than ever. I can say yes or no to jobs depending on how they'll affect my labour planning. I can say no to working with someone if our personalities clash.

However, taking annual leave is not something I'm comfortable doing often or for longer than a few days. I like to disconnect on holiday, and I'm usually unable to do that. I still respond to customer enquiries and often work while away to help solve urgent customer problems. So, I often turn down travel requests from friends and family if I think I may end up working.

As the face of the business, and as no one in the business shares my level of experience, delegating tasks is difficult. While I'm happy to admit I took my first holiday for longer than a week this year, taking time off for personal reasons is probably the most challenging aspect of running the business."

Running a small business is tough, especially when it seems you must do many different jobs. But it's important to realise the problems this 'doing it all' can cause and take steps to find a balance. Try to do this by getting help from others, focusing on what you're good at, managing your time well, learning continually, using technology, getting support from other business owners, and taking care of yourself. This not only helps your business succeed but also makes your life better, so you can thrive in the competitive market.

CHAPTER 5
HIGHLIGHTS

- ☑ **Financial Foundations**
- ☑ **Budgeting Basics**
- ☑ **Cash Flow Management**
- ☑ **Job Costing**
- ☑ **Pricing**
- ☑ **Financial Reporting**
- ☑ **Government Obligations**

CHAPTER 5
Mastering Money

Mastering money is essential for survival and growth. Without a solid grasp of your finances, your business can easily flounder, no matter how great your product or service may be. This chapter will guide you through the key principles and practices to help you take control of your business's finances, make informed decisions, and pave the way for long-term success.

Financial Foundations

It's crucial to establish a solid financial foundation for your small business. This foundation consists of three key elements:

Clear Financial Goals:

Start by setting clear financial goals for your business. What do you want to achieve financially in the short term, i.e. a quarter, and the long term, say one year? Are you looking to increase revenue, reduce expenses, or improve profitability?

Having specific, measurable goals will give you a sense of direction and purpose in managing your finances.

Accounting System:

Maintaining accurate financial records is non-negotiable. Implement an accounting system that works for your business, whether it's a simple spreadsheet or accounting software.

Keep track of all income and expenses, categorise them properly, and reconcile your accounts regularly. This will make it easier to monitor your financial health and prepare for end of financial year reporting.

Separate Personal and Business Finances:

One common mistake made by small business owners is mixing personal and business finances. So, it's ideal to open a dedicated business bank account and use it exclusively for your business transactions. This separation simplifies bookkeeping, prevents confusion, and ensures that you can easily track your business's financial performance.

In addition, I would always advise that you open a business savings account too. This is where the GST, PAYG and Superannuation savings will be kept, so that you can always meet your ATO and employer obligations.

Budgeting Basics

Once you've established your financial foundation, it's time to create a budget. Creating a budget is essential for managing your finances effectively and ensuring the long-term success of your business. Here are some simple steps to help you get started:

Set a Timeframe
Decide on the timeframe for your budget. Common choices are monthly, quarterly, or annually. The timeframe should align with your business's needs and planning cycle.

Estimate Revenue
Calculate your expected revenue for the budget period. This can include sales, investments, loans, or any other sources of income.

List your Expenses
Create a comprehensive list of all your business expenses. Categorise them into fixed (e.g., rent, salaries) and variable (e.g., utilities, supplies) expenses.

Monitor and Adjust: Regularly review your budget and compare it to your actual financial performance. If you're not meeting your goals or if unexpected expenses arise, adjust your budget accordingly.

James McCallister of The Good Creative said one of the biggest challenges he has found so far in his business was: *"Learning to watch vast amounts of money go out the door as quickly as it comes in – and remain calm about it - is something that takes some getting used to. Working hard and making good money is super rewarding, but the cost of business as you grow can be confronting. Once you learn to be pragmatic about it rather than emotional, things change."*

Free Budget template   EXAMPLE

Budget for Joe Bloggs Pty Ltd

	July		August		September	
	Budget	Actual	Budget	Actual	Budget	Actual
Income						
Sales 1	$100,000.00	$125,000.00	$100,000.00	$95,000.00	$150,000.00	$155,000.00
Sales 2	$25,000.00	$0.00	$10,000.00	$15,000.00	$10,000.00	$9,000.00
Sales 3	$30,000.00	$15,000.00	$10,000.00	$0.00	$10,000.00	$20,000.00
Sales 4	$25,000.00	$25,500.00	$30,000.00	$29,500.00	$30,000.00	$28,000.00
Total income	$180,000	$165,500	$150,000	$139,500	$200,000	$212,000
Expenses						
Rent	$6,000.00	$6,000.00	$6,000.00	$6,000.00	$6,000.00	$6,000.00
Printing	$200.00	$100.00	$200.00	$50.00	$200.00	$250.00

Here are my top tips for budgeting.

- Be honest about the purpose of your budget. The budget can be a very powerful sense-making tool if you approach it with honesty and discipline.

- It is hard to get your expenses exact. Overestimating the expenses allows for extra costs that you were not expecting.

- Trying to budget to the last penny and drilling it down will drive you crazy; this is not the objective of a budget.

- Businesses often keep their budgets secret. Sharing your budget with key employees can help with employee engagement.

- Your budget should be revisited and updated. The market is changing all the time, and your budget should reflect the changes that are happening in your business.

When I asked Justin Hillier from JCK Recruitment, "What lesson did you learn in your first few months of starting your new business?" he said:

"I cannot stress enough how critical planning is in business. Whether it's financial budgets, revenue forecasts, workforce management, or overall business strategies, it's imperative to have a solid plan in place.

Moreover, it's essential to be prepared with contingency plans and even backup plans for those contingencies. In the unpredictable world of business, your initial strategies may not always succeed. Maintaining discipline, particularly concerning budgets and expenditures, is paramount. If you're not cautious with your spending, it can quickly come back to haunt you. Staying within your financial limits and adhering to your budget is a crucial part of mastering money in business."

Cash Flow Management

Managing cash flow is critical for the survival of your small business. Cash flow is the movement of money in and out of your business, and it's the lifeblood of any organisation. Here's how to keep it flowing smoothly:

Monitor Receivables

Keep a close eye on your accounts receivable, which represents money owed to your business by customers or clients. Send invoices promptly, follow up on overdue payments, and consider offering discounts for early payments to encourage prompt settlement.

Control Payables

On the flip side, manage your accounts payable carefully. Negotiate favourable payment terms with suppliers, but don't delay payments past the agreed-upon terms, as this can harm your relationships and creditworthiness.

Build a Cash Reserve

Maintain a cash reserve specifically for managing daily operations. This reserve can help cover short-term expenses and ensure you have enough working capital to keep your business running smoothly.

Invest Wisely

If you have surplus cash, consider investing it wisely to generate additional income. Explore options such as money market accounts or short-term investments that offer liquidity and some degree of security.

Free Simple Cash Flow Forecast Tool

EXAMPLE

Cash flow for Joe Bloggs Pty Ltd

	October	November	December
OPENING CASH BALANCE	$35,000	$158,040	$372,880
Cash incoming			
Sales	$200,000.00	$250,000.00	$175,000.00
Asset sales	$0.00	$0.00	$0.00
Debtor receipts	$9,500.00	$6,000.00	$15,000.00
Government Grants	$0.00	$50,000.00	$0.00
Loans	$0.00	$0.00	$0.00
Other income	$300.00	$600.00	$750.00
Total incoming	$209,800.00	$306,800.00	$190,750.00
Cash outgoing			
Contractors	$10,000.00	$15,000.00	$7,500.00
Bank fees and charges	$10.00	$10.00	$10.00
Travel	$5,000.00	$5,000.00	$3,500.00
General Expenses	$3,000.00	$3,000.00	$2,000.00
Rent & rates	$6,000.00	$6,000.00	$6,000.00
Printing	$250.00	$250.00	$250.00
Income tax	$7,500.00	$7,500.00	$7,500.00
Wages & Superannuatic	$55,000.00	$55,000.00	$47,000.00
More...			
Total outgoing	$86,760	$91,760	$73,760

Pricing Strategies

Setting the right prices for your products or services is a delicate balance. Your prices need to cover your costs, generate profit, and remain competitive in the market. Consider these factors when determining your pricing strategy:

When Dylan Splatt of Cyclus was asked, "What is a valuable lesson you have learnt in your business?" He said, *"In hindsight, we realise the importance of perfecting our charge rate earlier on in our business. It took us 10 years to truly fine-tune it, but looking back, we wish we had prioritised this aspect from the very beginning."*

Cost Analysis

Calculate your cost per unit or service. Include all expenses, from materials and labour to overhead and marketing. Ensure your prices at least cover these costs to avoid operating at a loss.

Competitive Analysis

Research your competitors' pricing to understand where you stand in the market. Are you offering a premium product or service, or are you positioning yourself as a cost-effective option? Your pricing should align with your brand and target audience.

Value-Based Pricing

Consider the value your product or service provides to customers. Are you solving a significant problem or meeting a critical need? If so, you may be able to justify higher prices.

Test and Adjust

Don't be afraid to experiment with different price points. Monitor customer reactions and adjust your pricing strategy accordingly. It's an ongoing process that can lead to increased profitability.

Sophie Budd of Taste Budds Cooking Studio said, *"A valuable lesson I learnt was that the actual costs of outgoings were not just pie in the sky anymore; it was actual money and I had to make more than that to keep afloat."*

Debt Management

Debt can be a helpful tool for growing your business, but it must be managed wisely. Here are some guidelines for effective debt management:

Only Borrow What You Need

Borrowing should have a purpose, such as expanding your operations, purchasing inventory, or investing in marketing. Avoid borrowing for day-to-day expenses or non-essential purchases.

Shop for the Best Rates

When seeking loans or credit lines, compare offers from multiple lenders to secure the best terms and interest rates. A lower interest rate can significantly reduce the cost of borrowing.

Repayment Plan

Have a clear plan for repaying any debts you incur. Create a budget line item for loan payments which is a regular monthly amount, and stick to paying it. Early repayment whenever possible can save you money in interest.

Avoid Personal Guarantees

Whenever possible, avoid providing personal guarantees for business loans. This separates your personal assets from your business liabilities and protects your personal finances.

Financial Reporting and Analysis

Regular financial reporting and analysis are essential for making informed decisions and tracking your business's performance. Here's how to leverage financial statements effectively:

Profit & Loss Statement

Your profit and loss statement summarises your business's revenues, costs, and expenses over a specific period. It provides a snapshot of your profitability. Analyse it to identify areas where you can cut costs or increase revenue.

Balance Sheet

A balance sheet presents your business's financial position at a specific point in time, detailing your assets, liabilities, and equity. It helps you assess your business's overall financial health and solvency.

Cash Flow Statement

The cash flow statement tracks the movement of cash in and out of your business. It reveals how changes in your balance sheet and income statement affect your cash position. Monitor it closely to ensure you have enough liquidity to meet your obligations.

Key Performance Indicators (KPIs)

Identify and track key performance indicators relevant to your business. These might include customer payment days, customer lifetime value, gross profit margin, and inventory turnover rate. KPIs provide insights into your business's efficiency and effectiveness, and these are easy to set up in most business accounting dashboards.

In addition to your overall business reporting, it's also extremely important for you to understand and manage the costs associated with jobs/clients by breaking down the income and costs for each project.

Why is it Important to do Job Costing?

Getting the Right Price

You want to charge customers a fair price. Job costing helps you set the right price by making sure you cover all the costs and still make a profit.

Knowing the Winners and Losers

Some projects make more money than others. Job costing helps you figure out which projects are the money makers and which ones might be causing you to lose money.

Controlling Costs

It helps you keep an eye on spending. If costs are getting too high on a project, job costing lets you know so you can make adjustments, and avoid overspending.

Using Resources Smartly

You want to use your people and materials wisely. Job costing helps you see if you're using your resources efficiently or if there's a better way to get things done.

Avoiding Surprises

It's like having a financial crystal ball. Job costing helps you see any potential money problems before they happen, so you can plan ahead and avoid unpleasant surprises.

Telling the Money Story

With job costing, you can tell a clear money story to everyone interested in your business. This helps you show off your successes and make smart decisions for the future.

Plan for Taxes

Taxes can be a significant financial burden for small businesses, so tax planning is an integral part of mastering money for your small business. Here are some strategies to consider:

Consult a Tax Professional

Seek the advice of a qualified Accountant who specialises in small business. They can help you identify deductions, credits, and exemptions that apply to your business.

Understand Your Obligations

Know your tax obligations as a small business owner. This includes income tax, payroll tax, GST, and PAYG withholding tax.

Recordkeeping

Maintain meticulous records of all your income and expenses. There are many apps to help you track expense receipts. Proper documentation ensures you can claim all eligible deductions and credits.

Set Aside Tax Funds

Set aside your GST, PAYG, payroll tax and quarterly income

tax instalments. Pop the money into a business savings account which will ensure you have the money when the time comes around to pay for these costs.

Mastering money for your small business requires dedication, discipline, and ongoing effort. By establishing a solid financial foundation, budgeting effectively, managing cash flow, setting appropriate prices, handling debt wisely, analysing financial statements, and engaging in tax planning, you'll be well on your way to financial success.

Remember, financial management is a continuous process, and staying vigilant and adaptable will help your business thrive in the ever-changing world.

CHAPTER 6
HIGHLIGHTS

- ☑ **Justification for Hiring Staff**

- ☑ **Staffing Needs**

- ☑ **Reviewing Resumes**

- ☑ **Conducting Interviews**

- ☑ **Onboarding of Staff**

- ☑ **Employee Retention**

CHAPTER 6
Power to the People

Experiencing growth is an exciting time. It means your business is doing well, gaining popularity, and getting a bigger share of the market. However, growth can also be quite complicated. Eventually, you'll come to a point where there's more work to be done than you and/or your current team can handle.

Determining the right time to bring on a new employee can be challenging. While you recognise the need for assistance, hiring someone new is a huge commitment in time and money.

The big questions that may be holding you back from employing someone are: Is there enough work to justify hiring a new employee? How do I hire an employee? What are the rules and regulations? How do I train an employee?

How do I retain an employee? And how can I exit an employee if it's not working out?

Below are a few questions that you could ask yourself if you are looking to justify a new hire:

Justification

1. If you and your existing team are consistently overwhelmed with work, struggling to meet deadlines, or sacrificing work-life balance, it may be a sign that you need additional help. Analyse the workload to see what tasks can be delegated.

2. The quality of your product or service may be suffering due to a lack of time or resources, and this is where a new hire can maintain your quality standards.

3. Is your business financially stable enough to support a new hire? The costs of hiring a new employee can soon add up. It's not just salary costs; it's the advertising costs, the time spent looking over the resumes, interviewing, inducting, and training. All these processes cost time and money and need to be factored in. Will there be consistent money coming in to cover the salary on an ongoing basis?

Before you start the hiring process, it's essential to clearly define your staffing needs. The below areas of hiring staff could be your starting point.

Determine Your Staffing Needs

- What specific roles do you need to fill?

- How many employees do you need in each role?

- What qualifications and skills are required for each position?

- Do you need full-time, part-time, or casual employees?

- What's your budget?

Create Job Descriptions

Develop detailed job descriptions for each new position. These descriptions should include:

- Job title and responsibilities

- Qualifications and skills required

- Expected work hours and schedule

- Salary/Hourly rate

- Reporting structure and team dynamics

Attracting the Best Candidates

To attract potential employees, you can:

- Post job openings on your website, SEEK, Indeed and social media.

- Use professional networking platforms, like LinkedIn.

- Seek referrals from your existing staff and professional contacts.

- Consider using a recruiting agency for specialised roles.

Attracting the perfect candidate can sometimes be hard, as it's difficult to find people with the exact skills and workplace cultural fit. That's why some businesses are choosing to outsource work to people in other countries. This helps them access a wider talent pool and often saves money. Even though there are challenges, like dealing with time zone differences and cultural differences, outsourcing has become a popular way for businesses to get the right people for the job without breaking the bank.

When I was expanding my team, I was unsuccessful in finding a candidate who ticked all the boxes, so I decided to outsource. I used an outsourcing agency here in Perth to help find me a Senior Bookkeeper in the Philippines. The agency found eight candidates and I interviewed them using the same interview methods as I did when looking for someone local. The only difference was the interview was done over Zoom. The result? I ended up with a fantastic senior bookkeeper who has now been with me for almost 18 months, we have a great working relationship, she is very knowledgeable, highly skilled and she has a fantastic work ethic. I am so glad I chose her to work with me and my clients as it's a fantastic fit for *Precious Time*.

Review Resumes and Conduct Interviews

When you receive applications, you should carefully review the resumes and shortlist the candidates who meet your criteria. There should be a few who stand out.

Some Red Flags:

Unexplained gaps in employment history – When reviewing a candidate's work history, be wary of long breaks between jobs. While there might be a valid reason, like having a family or an illness, a serious candidate should be ready to explain these gaps during an interview.

Excessive job changes – Job hopping can show ambition, but too many changes in a short time may indicate a lack of commitment. While quick job switches can be for valid reasons, the resources spent on onboarding and training can be significant if the candidate is likely to repeat the pattern of switching jobs.

Lack of career progression – A resume with several jobs and no increase in responsibilities may suggest a lack of clear career direction or motivation.

Careless errors – With abundant online resources for resume writing, there's no excuse for a poorly organised or typo-ridden resume. Candidates who submit messy documents demonstrate a lack of attention to detail, which is a potential issue in most fields.

Irrelevant information – Having a couple of interesting hobbies showcasing relevant skills can make a candidate stand out. However, resumes that overly emphasise personal interests might suggest the job seeker is trying to fill space or views their career as a secondary pursuit.

In my years of experience, I've found that an important aspect of the interview process is assessing whether the candidate is a good cultural fit for the business. This involves ensuring that the prospective employee shares the same values, beliefs, and norms as your business.

A little note here: Remember that cultural fit is a two-way street. While you're assessing if the candidate fits your company culture, the candidate is also evaluating whether your company's culture aligns with their values and work style.

Here are some of my tips for conducting interviews:

- Ask questions that assess their qualifications and skills, including communication.

- Specifically address cultural fit. Ask them about their preferred work environment, how they handle challenges, and their values.

- Ask candidates about specific situations they've encountered in the past and how they handled them. This can provide insights into their behaviour and problem-solving skills.

- Evaluate the candidate's ability to adapt to different work environments and situations. This is especially important if your company experiences changes or has an ever-changing fast-paced work environment.

- Ensure that the candidate's career goals align with the company's mission and long-term objectives. This helps in determining whether they see themselves growing within the business.

When Mark Welsh of SMS Group Services was asked "What are some of the biggest challenges you face in your business today?" he replied with, *"Staff. The constant movement of staff in and out of the business is a significant challenge. Training employees only to lose them and having to repeat the process with new hires can be time-consuming and costly. The fluid nature of the job market in Perth makes recruitment challenging. The need to expand the recruitment department to handle the demands of labour requests has increased as the business has grown."*

To overcome these challenges, Mark said, *"Building a strong core team can help create a more stable and reliable workforce, as well as looking beyond local talent and considering offshore recruitment, including sponsoring skilled personnel from the UK. The key to overcoming the staffing challenges involves a combination of strategic hiring, talent retention initiatives and a proactive approach to addressing the demand of the dynamic job market in Perth."*

Whether you're an experienced employer or a new start up, the Interview Questions Tool can help to make your interviews run easily and smoothly, giving you the edge in finding candidates with the right skills, as well as being a good fit for your business. Adding your own questions which are derived from your values will help to ensure they are a good cultural fit.

Interview Questions Tool

Check References

Before making a final decision, contact the candidate's references to verify their work history and qualifications. This step is crucial in ensuring you hire trustworthy and reliable employees.

Make the Offer

Once you've identified the right candidate, extend a job offer. Be sure to outline the terms and conditions of employment, including salary, benefits, start date, and any other relevant details. Make sure to clarify any questions the candidate may have.

Onboarding and Training

After the candidate accepts your offer, it's time for onboarding and training. Provide new employees with all the necessary information, paperwork, and training they need to succeed in their roles. Ensure they understand your company's culture, values, and expectations.

Compliance

Although it can seem like quite a chore, it's important that you comply with all relevant employment laws and regulations when hiring staff. This includes issues related to minimum wage, overtime pay, worker's compensation and many more. Stay informed about local, state, and federal laws that affect your business.

It would be advisable to obtain some advice from a Human Resource Professional or contact the Fair Work Ombudsman. Take a look at the Fair Work Ombudsman website in order to keep on top of the forever-changing landscape of being an employer. Link: https://www.fairwork.gov.au/

Getting Help

Dylan Splatt of Cyclus Australia said that some of the biggest challenges they faced in the business so far was effective people management. To overcome this hurdle, they have surrounded themselves with exceptional consultants who share the Company's core values.

> *"By engaging the services of a skilled business coach and HR consultants, we have found invaluable support in navigating intricate people-related issues that arise during the operation and expansion of our business. We highly value having someone to rely on, so that our people feel heard, whilst we focus on growth."*

When thinking about hiring new staff in Australia, some key considerations of the compliance area, as well as the Fair Work Act 2009, are:

- Pay and Wages
- Leave
- Awards
- Employment Conditions
- Employee Rights and Obligations
- Ending Employment

When asked: "What's a valuable lesson you learnt from a mistake you made during your first year in business," Michael McCracken of Boss Carpentry said, *"To do things by the book. Early in my career, I sacked an employee in an incorrect way. His family had a business, and they lodged a complaint. I was investigated and fined. In addition, they found I had insufficient record-keeping (I had no Bookkeeper or any form of accounting system). This was the turning point for me and the real beginning of my business."*

Mike now has many staff working for him and runs two successful businesses.

Employee Retention

Keeping your team happy and engaged is just as crucial as hiring the right people. When you invest in retaining staff, you're investing in the stability and success of your business. Here are some simple steps to help keep your team motivated and committed for the long haul:

Create a Positive Work Environment

Foster a workplace culture where employees feel valued and supported. Encourage open communication, recognise achievements, and provide constructive feedback. A positive atmosphere goes a long way in retaining happy and motivated staff.

Promote Work-Life Balance

Respect your employees' time outside of work. Promote a healthy work-life balance by setting realistic expectations, avoiding excessive overtime, and encouraging employees to take breaks. This helps prevent burnout and keeps morale high.

Invest in Professional Development

Support your team's growth by offering training and development opportunities. This not only enhances their skills but also shows that you're committed to their long-term success. A workforce that sees a future within your company is more likely to stay.

Recognise and Reward

Acknowledge hard work and dedication through regular recognition and rewards. This could be as simple as a shout-out in a team meeting, a small bonus, or other incentives. Feeling appreciated boosts morale and strengthens the bond between your team and the company.

Provide Career Pathways

Help your employees see a future with your business by offering clear career paths. Discuss growth opportunities, promotions, and how their role contributes to the overall success of the company. A sense of purpose and progression keeps employees invested.

Listen and Act on Feedback

Regularly seek feedback from your team and take actionable steps to address concerns. This demonstrates that you value their input and are committed to making positive changes based on their experiences and suggestions.

Hiring staff for a small business is a critical process that directly affects its success. From crafting clear job descriptions to leveraging cost-effective recruitment channels and technology, each step plays a vital role. Thorough and process-driven interviews, and assessing both skills and cultural fit, will ensure the right match. The onboarding process is key for seamless integration, and here is a reminder of the importance of aligning new hires with company values.

In the dynamic small business environment, adaptability is crucial. Investing in ongoing training and development not only retains talent but also fosters continuous growth.

Ultimately, the quality of a small business's workforce is central to its success. By strategically approaching hiring as an investment, small businesses can build a team that meets immediate needs while contributing to long-term sustainability. With an intentional hiring process, small businesses position themselves for resilience and growth in the face of challenges. Navigating the competitive landscape is also easier with a dynamic and skilled team.

This chapter has only lightly touched on the topic of employees as it's such a complex area, but I hope it has been enough to provide you with some of the basics.

Always make sure that you seek advice from either an Employment Lawyer or a Human Resources professional before hiring staff.

Embarking on the journey of understanding employment intricacies is a bit like setting out on a road trip; it's wise to have a reliable map (or expert advice in this case) and perhaps a good playlist (employment policies and employee handbook). After all, every journey is better with a bit of guidance.

CHAPTER 7
HIGHLIGHTS

☑ **Embracing Change**

☑ **Positive Mindset**

☑ **Building Resilience**

☑ **Closing a Business**

CHAPTER 7
When Life Throws You a Curve Ball

Life is unpredictable, and the world of small business is no exception. Just when you think you have everything under control, a curve ball comes hurtling your way. It might be a sudden economic downturn, a global pandemic, or a technological shift. Regardless of the nature of the curve ball, your ability to adapt and stay resilient will determine the fate of your small business.

Embracing Change

Change is inevitable in every business, and sometimes it comes at you with unexpected speed and force. The key to success is not avoiding these curve balls but for you to learn how to hit them out of the park.

See below my top tips for embracing changes in your business.

Assess the Situation

When life throws you a curve ball, step back and assess the situation. What exactly has changed, and how does it impact your business? Understanding the scope and nature of the challenge will enable you to formulate an effective response.

Adaptability is the Name of the Game

In a rapidly-changing world, adaptability is a small business owner's greatest asset. The ability to adapt quickly can mean the difference between survival and failure. Be prepared to pivot your business model, reassess your target audience, or explore new revenue streams.

Darren McFarlane of Next Level Mentoring told me of how he had to adapt when he was thrown many curve balls in his business. *"My most challenging period occurred last year in my business. It was a dark time in my life and a turning point that affected me deeply.*

Despite my excitement about leaving my job and dedicating myself fully to my business, things took an unexpected turn. The financial strain became apparent, and what was meant to be a celebratory transition turned into a sombre occasion. My Father became ill and passed away; shortly after, my Mum faced health issues, breaking her knee and requiring my immediate attention in the UK. Meanwhile, my daughter also suffered a knee fracture, adding to the complexities.

The emotional toll and the responsibilities of caring for my family disrupted my business momentum. I had to redirect my focus, attending to my Mum's needs and supporting my daughter during her recovery.

Financially, the strain intensified as I spent a significant amount on flights back to the UK due to COVID-related disruptions. The funds I had saved for my business plans quickly dwindled. Despite the setbacks, I made a crucial decision not to give up on my business entirely. I acknowledged the necessity of finding a job for immediate financial stability but remained committed to reapproaching my business differently. Reflecting on these darkest moments, I recognised the strength gained from enduring such challenges. Rather than succumbing to despair, I embraced a resilient mindset and committed to rebuilding my business with a renewed perspective."

Cultivate a Positive Mindset

We can all rebound from curveballs with a positive outlook. Having a thoughtful and consistent approach, you can foster a culture that sees change as an opportunity rather than a threat, and encourage employees to adopt a positive and open mindset towards new ideas and processes.

Effective Communication

Clearly communicate the reasons behind the change, keeping everyone informed about the benefits and potential challenges. Then address concerns and provide a platform for open dialogue. This may entail a quick 10-minute stand up scrum meeting every morning.

Create a Change Management Plan

Develop a well-structured change management plan outlining the steps and timelines. Identify potential obstacles and strategise how to overcome them.

Celebrate Small Wins

Acknowledge and celebrate achievements and milestones during the change process by recognising individuals or teams that contribute to the successful implementation of changes.

Lead by Example

Demonstrate your commitment to change by embracing it yourself. Leaders who actively support and participate in the change process set a positive example for others.

Learn from Mistakes amid Change

Understand that not all changes will go smoothly or be the right path. Use setbacks as learning opportunities to refine your strategies for future changes.

Tim Lewis, Founder of Safestyle Pty Ltd, said:

"I make mistakes every day! But I try to focus on all the good we are creating. Some years ago, I had an issue with some stock and had to discard 5000 pairs of protective eyewear. This was quite a stressful time as it was a lot of money gone to waste. I tried to recycle the 5000 pairs, but it turned out no one would recycle them even though they were made from recyclable polycarbonate. So, I went surfing and cleared my mind, and once I returned to work, we had an idea to start up SafeStyle Recycling, a program designed to recycle all brands of protective eyewear. This is now in progress, and we have collection bins on mine sites and expanding into retail stores Australia wide.

Not all mistakes and problems can be turned into a positive overnight, but if I am faced with problems or make mistakes, I've learnt to keep calm, take a breath and try my best to find the positive in each situation. I feel everything happens for a reason…."

Tim pivoted and turned a problem into something that could be another revenue stream in the coming year.

Building Resilience

Building resilience is crucial for you to navigate the challenges and uncertainties that come your way. If you cultivate resilience in business and in yourself, you are better equipped to weather storms and emerge stronger on the other side. A resilient business fosters a positive work environment, boosting employee morale and retention, even during tough times.

Below are my top tips on building resilience:

Diversify Revenue Streams

Relying on a single source of income can be risky. Explore new products, services, or markets to diversify your revenue streams.

Mark Welsh from SMS Group Services has many years under his belt and knows only too well about diversifying. He said, "When setbacks happen, like losing a client or valuable team members, it feels awful for the first 48 hours. After that initial tough period, you start thinking about other possibilities. By the middle of the week, you realise the impact isn't as massive as it seemed. I've experienced losing significant contracts twice in business, and the key difference lies in having more experienced managerial people on board. The collaboration of the leadership team allows us to strategise together and, in essence, diversify. We have ensured diversification by expanding our client base from two major clients to having seven or eight. Diversifying is crucial in business, as it adds strength and resilience."

Financial Planning and Management

Maintain a strong financial plan with a focus on cash flow management. Having a financial buffer can help your business survive lean periods.

Invest in Technology

Embrace new technology to streamline operations and enhance efficiency. This can improve your ability to adapt to changing market conditions.

Build Strong Relationships

Develop strong relationships with customers, suppliers, and other businesses. These networks can provide support and collaboration opportunities during challenging times.

Employee Training and Wellbeing

Invest in training programs to boost your employees' skills. Also, prioritise their wellbeing to ensure a motivated and committed workforce.

Risk Management

Identify potential risks and develop strategies to mitigate them. This includes having a comprehensive insurance plan tailored to your business's needs.

Strategic Planning

Develop a flexible and forward-looking business strategy. Regularly review and adjust your plans based on the evolving business landscape.

Learn from Setbacks

Treat setbacks as learning opportunities. Analyse what went wrong, make necessary adjustments, and use the experience to strengthen your business.

Dan Bailey from Tradie HQ said, *"There is no point worrying about something that you can't change. So work out what you can influence and concentrate on improving those. Personally, I approach challenges with objectivity, whether it's facing rejection or when things don't go to plan. I try to extract positives from every situation, no matter how disastrous it may seem. There's always a takeaway, be it a valuable lesson for the future or a new perspective on tackling a problem."*

Community Engagement

Engage with your local community. Building strong ties can provide mutual support during challenging times.

Adopt a Positive Mindset

Foster a positive and resilient mindset within your team. A 'can do' attitude can make a huge difference in overcoming obstacles.

Yara Founder of The Yoga Studio had to build resilience when the Covid-19 pandemic hit. When asked, "What are some of the biggest challenges you have faced so far in business?" she answered:

"Covid challenged me the most. Running our business through lockdowns and mandates was not that much of a financial challenge as the government evened out any losses. The emotional ramifications took a toll on us. Even with the government's financial help, the emotional toll was a much bigger challenge. Running a community-orientated Yoga Studio where one of the key values is human connection, lockdowns, mandates and last-minute governmental changes presented themselves as challenges we were not prepared for.

Whereas others got to enjoy the 'perks' of working from home, our workload doubled, if not tripled – unlike our revenue. We had to change our entire business model and move our classes online, work out a way of supporting our teaching team, and all of this within a very short timeframe. However, there was also the beauty that came with the mess: the support of our community warmed our hearts. The love and support that our community showed us definitely helped move us through the tough times of Covid with more ease."

When it's Time to say Goodbye

Sometimes even when you have tried your hardest, spent a lot of money and tried to be innovative, the writing may be on the wall that it is time to close the business down. Closing a small business can be a difficult and emotionally challenging process. It's easy to feel down about it but it's really no different to any other learning experience in life.

If you find yourself in a situation where you need to close your business, it's important to approach the process with care and attention to various aspects.

Assess the Financial Situation

Review your financial statements to understand the extent of the financial challenges.

Speak with your Accountant and Financial Advisors

Identify outstanding debts, liabilities, and obligations.

Communicate with Stakeholders

Notify employees, suppliers, customers, and other stakeholders as early as possible.

Be transparent and honest about the reasons for closing. Many people have 'walked a mile in your shoes' and would completely understand.

Legal Considerations

Consult with legal professionals to understand the legal requirements for closing a business in your State.

Fulfill any outstanding legal obligations and get your Accountant and Bookkeeper to help with any outstanding lodgements with the ATO.

Employee Considerations

Consult with your Human Resources provider.

Provide clear information to employees about the closure and the timeline.

Comply with Fair Work regarding notice periods, severance pay, and other employee rights.

Inventory and Assets

Create an inventory of business assets and determine how they will be liquidated or sold. For a shop, sometimes stock can be sold at a discount at the markets, for instance.

Consider selling other assets to help cover outstanding debts.

Debts and Liabilities

Communicate with creditors and work on a plan to settle outstanding debts.

Prioritise payments based on urgency and legal obligations.

Customer Communication

Inform customers about the closure and of any impact on services or product availability.

Provide information on how they can retrieve deposits, if applicable.

Financial Assistance

Investigate government programs or financial assistance options that may be available to help during the closure process.

Personal Support

Seek emotional support from friends, family, or support groups.

Take care of your mental and physical health during this challenging time.

> *An anonymous contact of mine had this to say about his business which, after only a couple of years, he had to close: "I started a small boutique gym in November 2019. Previously to my first business venture I had been a gym manager and instructor, and a personal trainer for 5 years. I was so used to always being on a salary and yet I decided it was time for a change and make things happen! I had this dream about having my own gym (everything under one roof) Strength classes, Fitness classes & Yoga classes. I had made a business plan and had been looking for a few locations but had no experience in running a business whatsoever. I just had a strong belief in myself and my knowledge and capabilities. So, after finding investors, I managed to pull together $40,000 and that was enough for me to start on.*

> *I searched for locations and small gyms and finally found a location in Balcatta, WA. The place was listed as a 'warehouse' zoning wise, so before I could open up, the landlord and I had to get Change of Use through Stirling Council. That took a while but after a lot of work with building surveyors, architects and constantly contacting the council to speed things up, I was now in business.*

I did everything myself in the beginning, until I could afford to hire three instructors. After 2.5 to 3 years in business, I wasn't going anywhere! I was just breaking even. Plus, I wanted to start a family. So, sadly, I had to send out the hard news to my members and clients that we were closing. I luckily managed to sell the business (on a slight loss) but still had the lease for the building that I needed to honour. We then worked out with the landlord and real estate agents that he could take over the lease.

I don't regret starting my business, because the things I have learned from the 2-3 years of having it were extremely valuable. I grew stronger from the pressured decisions that had to be made and the hard times... as well as the feeling of accomplishment of making it all happen, and meeting and helping a lot of amazing people, including making many friends."

Remember, the decision to close a business is not a sign of failure. It can be a practical choice in response to changing market conditions, personal circumstances, or other factors. Learning from the experience can help you in future endeavours. If possible, consider seeking advice from business mentors or industry experts who may provide valuable insights.

On the rollercoaster ride of running a small business, those surprise curveballs that life throws at us can be really tough, but, as you have read from some of my clients, they tackled these challenges. They adapted where they could, they changed their mindsets, and they learnt from their mistakes.

In the world of small business, it's all about facing surprises with a 'can do' attitude. You can't freak out when things get tough. Roll with the punches, come up with new ideas, and learn from the challenges. Be ready to change, have good people to lean on, and don't give up too easily when things get rough – these are the keys to making it through the twists and turns of running a small business.

CHAPTER 8
HIGHLIGHTS

- ☑ **Understanding the Struggles of Work and Life**

- ☑ **Taking Care of Yourself**

- ☑ **Delegation**

- ☑ **Setting SMART Goals**

- ☑ **Support Systems**

CHAPTER 8
Taking Care of Yourself

Understanding the Struggles

Running a small business is exciting, but let's be real – it's not all rainbows and sunshine. There are days when the stress piles up, and you feel like you're juggling a million things at once. That's why I thought it important to share some simple but effective ways to keep your wellbeing in check as you navigate the world of small business.

Balancing Act: Work and Life

Running a small business can often feel like being on call 24/7. It's like being the superhero of your own story... but even superheroes need a break. I know I do. Finding a balance between work and your personal life is like mastering a recipe - it might take some trial and error, but it's worth it in the end.

Why is this so important? Well, when you're constantly on the go, it's easy to burn out. Your creativity dwindles, decision making becomes a chore, and suddenly, what was once your passion project feels like a never-ending to-do list.

How do you find balance? Start by setting clear boundaries, which I know is far easier said than done! Designate specific times for work and personal life. When it's work time, focus entirely on that. When it's personal time, give yourself permission to unplug. It could be a family dinner, a hobby you enjoy, or simply chilling on the couch with a good book. The key is to create mental and physical spaces for both aspects of your life.

Now put it into practice:

Designate Work Hours

Treat your business like a 9-to-5 job. Of course, there will be times when you need to go above and beyond, but having a general daily routine can prevent work from seeping into every corner of your life.

Technology Detox

Set specific times to check emails and messages. Constant notifications can make it feel like work is always looming. Give yourself the gift of uninterrupted downtime.

Prioritise Family and Personal Time

Whether it's a weekend getaway, a family dinner, or a solo hike, make sure to schedule moments that are just for you and your loved ones. These moments recharge your emotional batteries and keep you connected to the reasons you started your business in the first place.

Tim Lewis of Safestyle explained how he looks after his wellbeing and what he'd suggest for other busy owners. He said, *"Keeping a balance of work and play is the main thing that affects me. I love my work, but I also love my weekends. I love the ocean and every activity you can do with it. So, I make sure I get to the beach as often as I can to either go for a run with my dog, surf, kitesurf, fish, dive, or even just go watch the sunset and relax. I'm also lucky enough to surround myself with great family and friends, but I do love my alone time to recharge... I feel that the balance with allowing yourself to take some personal time is really important. I love to also have a little adventure to look forward to, as it's always great for peace of mind, whether that's a camp trip north or south, or an overseas trip. It doesn't matter how far out it is, just look forward to escaping the daily routine. I love my job and the team so much, so every day is exciting and uplifting. So many people get stuck in a job that they don't enjoy and feel they can't escape. And lastly, eat well, set aside time for regular exercise, and enjoy a few beers with your close ones regularly."*

Me Time

First things first — take care of yourself

You're the heart and soul of your business, and when you feel good physically, it's like putting on your superhero cape for the day.

Why does this matter? It's simple – a healthy you is a productive you. When you're physically fit, you have more energy, better focus, and improved resilience against stress. Me time isn't selfish; it's an investment in your business and your overall happiness.

Putting 'Me time' into practice:

Exercise Regularly

You don't need to become a fitness guru overnight. A simple walk, a quick home workout, or even stretching can do wonders. Find an activity you enjoy and make it a part of your routine.

Quality Sleep

Sleep is the unsung hero of wellbeing. Aim for 7-9 hours of quality sleep each night. It's during sleep that your body and mind recharge, setting you up for a productive day.

Healthy Eating Habits

Your body is your business's headquarters. Give it the right fuel. Ensure your diet includes a mix of fruits, vegetables, lean proteins, and whole grains. Avoid excessive caffeine and sugar, which can lead to energy crashes.

When I asked Andrew Dennehy of Plannet32 what he did to look after his wellbeing, he said, *"There's probably two main things: I train in Brazilian Jujitsu, which is a great way to relieve stress because it's something you have to focus 100% on when you're doing it. So regardless of how bad the day has been, when you go and get training and you start sparring or grappling with people, you have to focus 100% on that. And so that helps you get out a bit of aggression. Let's say that you're internalising, but it also means you have to turn your thoughts off completely because you can't be thinking about, you know, spreadsheets when you're trying not to die. So that helps a lot. But the thing I've discovered recently, which has become a huge part of my life very quickly, is Surf Lifesaving. So I started doing Surf Lifesaving and it's opened up a whole new set of skills, opportunities – a whole new social circle that is completely separate from work. And so that's been great. That's been a real, you know, physical and mental boost."*

Team Power

You don't have to be a one-person show. Delegate tasks to your team or consider outsourcing. Trust me, it takes a load off your plate and lets you focus on what you do best.

Why is delegation essential? Many small business owners fall into the trap of trying to do everything themselves. The result? Burnout, stress, and a business that's not reaching its full potential. Delegating tasks isn't a sign of weakness; it's a strategic move to ensure the success and sustainability of your business.

How do you delegate effectively?

Identify Your Strengths

What are the tasks that you excel at? What are the aspects that truly require your expertise? Identify these and focus on them. Delegating doesn't mean handing over the reins entirely; it means strategically distributing tasks.

Build a Reliable Team

Surround yourself with a reliable and skilled team. Whether it's full-time employees, freelancers, or consultants, having a team you can trust is key to effective delegation.

Effective Communication

Clearly communicate expectations, deadlines, and any specific requirements. Regular check-ins ensure that everyone is on the same page.

Goals, Bit by Bit

Setting goals doesn't mean aiming for the moon right away. Break down your big dreams into smaller, doable tasks. Celebrate the wins, no matter how small — it's like giving yourself a high-five.

Why are goals important? Goals provide direction and purpose. They're the road map that guides your business forward. However, setting unrealistic or overwhelmingly large goals can lead to frustration and burnout. By breaking down your objectives into manageable tasks, you create a sense of accomplishment and progress.

How do you set and achieve goals?

SMART Goals

Make your goals Specific, Measurable, Action-oriented, Realistic, and Time-bound. This framework ensures that your goals are clear, realistic, and actionable.

Nail that Goal

Prioritise Tasks

Not all tasks are created equal. Identify the high impact tasks that contribute most to your goals and tackle them first. This prevents the feeling of being overwhelmed by a long to-do list.

Celebrate Milestones

Each small victory is a step toward your larger goal. Take the time to acknowledge and celebrate these milestones. It's a powerful motivator and yet a lot of people in business forget to do this.

Money Mindset

Money stress is a common problem, although with courage, you can tackle it head on. In Chapter 5 we talked about creating a budget and knowing financial statements, but you should also explore ways to save and perhaps discuss with a bookkeeper, accountant or a financial counsellor.

Taking control of your finances reduces the stress, and that's a win-win.

Why does a healthy money mindset matter?

Financial worry can seep into every aspect of your life. It affects decision-making, relationships, and overall wellbeing. By adopting a positive money mindset and implementing sound financial practices, you not only secure the financial health of your business but also alleviate a significant source of stress.

How do you develop a healthy money mindset?

Create a Budget
Track your income and expenses. A budget provides a clear picture of your financial situation and allows you to make informed decisions.

Emergency Fund

Establishing an emergency fund provides a financial safety net. It reduces anxiety about unexpected expenses and provides peace of mind.

Seek Professional Advice

If finance isn't your forte, don't hesitate to seek the expertise of an accountant or financial advisor. They can offer insights, identify potential savings, and help you make informed financial decisions.

Buddy System

You don't have to be alone in this journey. Build a support crew – other business pals, mentors, or friends who get it. Sharing experiences and seeking advice can make the road less bumpy.

Why is having a support system important?

Running a small business can be lonely. Having a support system provides a network of understanding individuals who can offer advice, encouragement, and sometimes just a listening ear. It's a powerful tool for navigating challenges and celebrating successes.

How do you build and leverage your support system?

Mentorship

Seek out mentors who are in small business. This can be someone in the same profession or not. Their guidance can be invaluable, offering insights and perspectives gained through their own experiences.

Networking Events

Attend local or online networking events to connect with fellow entrepreneurs. Share your experiences freely and learn from others facing similar challenges.

Online Communities

Join online forums or social media groups related to your industry. Engage with others, ask questions, and contribute to the community. Think of it as a virtual watercooler where you can share your victories and vent your frustrations.

Dan Bailey from Tradie HQ said, *"At one point in the start-up phase of Tradie HQ, my wife and I were managing another 3 businesses as well as juggling family life and that certainly caused some stress and emotional struggles. It is important to have a support system, surround yourself with like-minded people. Even here at Tradie HQ just having casual chats at the coffee machine, even if it's not focused on problems, just a quick chat can uplift your mood. Seeking professional help from a therapist is also a good idea; it's like consulting a coach or an accountant for business matters. Engaging with a mental health professional provides an objective perspective and you get some valuable feedback."*

Tech Magic

Technology isn't just for big corporations. Embrace software tools that make your life easier – whether it's automating tasks or using apps for smoother communication. It's like having a little helper in your pocket.

Why is technology your friend?

In the age of digital advancement, there is now a huge range of tools designed to simplify and enhance various aspects of your business. For instance, keeping in touch with clients, having video calls with your remote team, organising your daily tasks, and project management, just to name a few. Leveraging technology can save you time, reduce stress, and boost overall efficiency in your business.

What tech tools can you use to make business easier?

Project Management Software

Tools like Trello, Asana, or Monday.com can help you organise tasks, set deadlines, and collaborate with your team seamlessly.

Communication Apps

Slack, Microsoft Teams, or even WhatsApp can streamline communication, reducing the clutter in your inbox.

Automation Platforms

Platforms like Zapier or Integromat allow you to automate repetitive tasks. Linking up your apps in Zapier to do something as simple as saving any attachments in emails to your Google Drive can free up your time for more strategic activities.

Learn as You Go

Lastly, keep the learning vibes alive. Attend workshops and webinars, or just pick up a book. Growing your skills not only helps your business but it gives you a sense of accomplishment.

Why is continuous learning crucial? The business landscape is ever evolving. Stagnation can lead to your expertise or product offering not being up to date. By embracing a mindset of continuous learning, you not only stay relevant in your industry but also fuel your personal growth.

How can you incorporate continuous learning into your routine?

Online Courses

Platforms like Udemy, Coursera, or LinkedIn Learning offer a wide range of courses on various topics. Pick a course that aligns with your business goals or explores a new skill.

Industry Events

Attend conferences, workshops, and webinars relevant to your industry. Not only do you gain insights, but you also have the opportunity to network with like-minded individuals.

Read Widely

Books are a treasure trove of knowledge. Make reading a habit, whether it's business books, industry journals, or even book summaries. Reading broadens your perspective and keeps your mind engaged.

Taking care of yourself in the small business landscape is a priority. Enhancing mental and physical wellbeing can help contribute to greater success in your business. Small business owners who integrate self care into their routines position themselves as resilient leaders, ready to face challenges with creativity.

Ultimately, investing in personal wellbeing not only ensures the longevity of the business but also enhances the overall fulfillment of the entrepreneur. Find that balance, embrace support, and remember, you're not just building a business; you're building a life.

PEARLS OF WISDOM

As you navigate your way to either start a small business or grow the small business you already have, I think it's useful for you to have some real-life pearls of wisdom from some of my past and current clients. I hope that these will help you on your journey in your small business.

I asked my clients, *What is the one piece of advice you would give someone thinking of starting a business or for someone already in business?* Here is what some had to say:

Andrew Dennehy - Plannet32: "Has to be two parts. So, one is just do it. I procrastinated for a while about doing it, but it's very easy to start to form a company; the forming of a company and registering the ABN is a doddle. And there are services online that can help you to do that. But the second part would be consider not doing it all by yourself. See if there are other people who you can work with, who you can trust, and who have a similar motivation; work together and you're going to find it a lot easier."

Darren McFarlane - Next Level Mentoring: "Just start it, just start the process. Because once you do, it's all about momentum. Take the analogy of the plane taking off using all the fuel, but once it's up, it uses less fuel. We've just got to start now because if you were to wait for the perfect conditions, they would never happen. And the second bit of advice is always remember that a great idea poorly executed will fail but an ok idea well executed will succeed. So it's not about the idea and the perfection of the idea. It's actually the execution of the idea that will stand you out. I know many people who give up and I know many people haven't even started. I've had many conversations, 'the graveyard ideas' as I call them. These people simply don't do anything, or they only do a little bit and then stop, so the business doesn't even get off the ground. You just have to keep going."

Dr Ian Dunican - Melius Consulting: "I think some people think because you own a business you must be loaded but its not the case in those first months, but people may go into it thinking that they are going to have lots of money. Don't do it to make money. If you think you're going to start a business and take money out of it in the first year, forget about it. It's going to be 12 to 18 months before you can do that. You are probably going to have to put a heap of money into the business first to get started.

So, if you don't have the financial means to go into business, don't do it. Likewise, don't realign your expectations and say, *I'm going to live off 25% of my income.* That won't work. On the upside, there will hopefully be times down the line when you are making a profit and can take money out."

Mark Welsh – SMS Group Services: "Do your homework first and get everything set up properly. From an accounting point of view, from a bookkeeping point of view, legally, set all the processes up, and talk to people who are in business and get some really, good advice. Having everything in order in the first place, will be a time-saving exercise, rather than having to go back and start again. Depending on how big your team can be, surround yourself with really good people and try not to employ anyone you know. If you are not happy with an employee, don't hang onto them; it's the hardest thing to do to let them go but it's for the best. And don't re-employ people who have been disgruntled."

Tanya Pavez – Magnetic People: "Go with your gut; it's always right. If it doesn't feel right, it's not right. I just absolutely knew that I could build this business up. It takes a lot of courage, but I knew that I would make it successful no matter what."

Alexander Blain – Retired: "If you fail to plan, you plan to fail."

Dylan Splatt – Cyclus: "Embrace the leap! Owning a business offers a remarkable sense of freedom and fulfilment when managed well. If you're considering a service-based venture, gain confidence and knowledge by starting with volunteering opportunities while still in your 'day job.' For those pursuing a product-based business, prioritise drafting a Non-Disclosure Agreement (NDA) and collaborate with a company that can help bring your initial product idea to life, before venturing out on your own. Take small steps, learning to trust your instincts as you progress. Remember, it's natural to experience imposter syndrome, so don't let it deter you."

Trent Stevens – Perth Formwork Stripping: "My piece of advice for anyone wanting to start a business is to first of all get all your insurances for the staff, business and yourself. You don't want to be without it when it's needed."

Steve: "Really think extremely hard about your decision first. Think everything through. Make a business plan; think where you want to be in the future. Have a strong reason for why you want to do it. See if you can get it started with someone you trust. Make a budget and have a strong brand or niche that can set you apart from everyone else. Think hard about the agreements you're about to make (i.e., loans, deals, rental agreements, etc.)."

Sophie Budd – Taste Budds Cooking Studio: "Think it through properly, see who else is doing what you do, ask advice from other business."

Sacha Fulton - Peak Preparation: "If you are going to start a business set it up as efficiently as you can from the start, so you can invest your precious time into stuff that requires you to drive it. Anything that can be automated and driven by a computer then do it."

Christine Tinley - Guides 4 Sight: "It was so easy to get swept up in the hype and drama of the industry and other people's expectations. For me, the most important thing was being very clear about my own core beliefs about how I wanted to develop my business and culture with staff, clients and the industry. I had to keep reminding myself that this was my business, and 'I could do this my way'."

Yara Kuehn - The Yoga and Pilates Room Scarborough: "Listen to your heart, take calculated risks and don't listen to the opinions of others, especially not when they are driven by their own personal fears. There are many things I would not have done if I hadn't trusted my own gut. Allow yourself to make mistakes, stay humble and ask for help when needed. If you can afford it, get yourself an accountant, a bookkeeper (one of the best things I've done!) and a lawyer. Delegate tasks that are out of your own field of expertise and focus on those parts of the business that you enjoy working on. Trust the people that want the best for you. Bottom line: there are many things and 'parameters' that we have control over while running a business - just don't get hung up on the things that are outside of your control."

Anonymous: "Recognise what sets you apart from other businesses in your field and make it your selling point. If you struggle to identify that, consider what you can do to make it work, but it won't be an easy process. Owning your own business is really tough and requires A LOT more work than you'd probably expect. The easiest way to be successful is to keep moving forward and to offer something different to what is out there or 'the norm'."

Aldo Sal Margio - Cyclus: "Starting a business and going out on your own is very exciting when it begins, but it starts to become stressful as you evolve and are more self-reliant, and it becomes more demanding. And the pressure builds when you have people who depend on you and the decisions that you make.

There are two things I would be certain of before starting a business: The first at a minimum is making sure you have a passion for what you are doing. When you love what you do and you are doing it for yourself, it doesn't matter how much time you spend doing it; it's not work – it's just what you do. My second tip is to not do it alone. Having someone by your side when the going gets tough is crucial, and when things are good, it's better to celebrate those wins with someone. Starting a business shouldn't be a short-term goal, the freedom and flexibility of having your own business is really a balancing act, and having someone on your side who you can support and vice versa makes it so much more rewarding."

Michael McCracken - Boss Carpentry WA: "Stick to what you know, do it really well, train people in that same thing, then start to diversify. Be good with Money BEFORE going out on your own. If you can't save money on your current income, don't think having your own business will make it any better. Build in safety nets (money); have multiple accounts (tax, super, insurances)."

James McAllister - The Good Creative: "Make sure you love what you do. You can't just pretend to love it, it won't work. You have to really love it. You have to be prepared to live and breathe it, day in, day out for years and years and years on end. You need to roll your sleeves up and rip in over an extended period of time you have to be in love with the process... not just the idea of it working out in the end. If you can do that with a smile on your face, you'll go far."

Alex Toyne - Toyne & Associates: "Talk to people. People will be your most important source of future opportunities, personal growth, professional development and innovation in your industry. Also, seek advice on all aspects of your business. Talk to bookkeepers and accountants to set up the administrative side of your business correctly so that it supports you rather than hinders you."

Rachel Huber - Bare Digital: "If you're considering launching a business, start by seeking informal mentors with their own businesses. Message your friends who have successful businesses, and ask them if you can pick their brains because you'd appreciate their advice (over a beer or meal to sweeten the deal). People like to help others, and your request validates that you consider them knowledgeable and trustworthy. While their situation may differ, it helps to have people who can empathise with your situation, that you can talk to, bounce ideas off and seek guidance from. Topics that may seem confusing and overwhelming at first, like GST or managing tax, can be broken down into small, easily digestible knowledge bombs by people who've been there before. Others may have great suppliers to recommend. You'll likely find someone you click with - they may have the same risk appetite, budget or management style, and you'll have a valuable business mentor to turn to when needed."

Luke Hall - Eaton Hall: "To just do it. Too many people procrastinate and focus on the negatives. My view is that later in life, very few people are going to think 'I wish I hadn't started that business', but quite a few are going to think 'I wish I had started that business'. Starting a business is scary, exciting, tiring, and full of lots of other emotions, but it is super rewarding, and gives you the opportunity to develop lifelong relationships and a sense of achievement. It is super empowering."

Tim Lewis - Safestyle: "My advice is to focus on your own business and not worry about what anyone else is doing. Sure, use other brands and businesses as motivation, but stay your course and set big goals. Be open to meeting new people and engage with mentors or people who have been in similar shoes, as this will fast track your skills and understanding faster than anything. And lastly, learn to let go of control once you can afford it, and build a likeminded team that all share the same mission, vision and more importantly values. Oh, and keep a sustainable balance of work and play. This is incredibly important if you want to enjoy the ride and create a healthy sustainable business."

And finally, my own advice is very similar to most of the above: Do your research but don't take too long or it will never get off the ground. Surround yourself with the right people who can help you succeed in the set up and ongoing ups and downs of business, like accountants, lawyers, bookkeepers, insurance brokers, mentors, and HR professionals. And, of course, make sure you have the support of your family and friends, as it's going to be one hell of a bumpy ride.

The Next Steps

And there you have it – the end of this journey. This book isn't just me lecturing you and then throwing in a few stories for effect. It's your down-to-earth handbook, your cheat sheet and your secret weapon designed to help you navigate your journey into the small business world. Learning from my clients' stories, the step-by-step guides and practical advice can help you dodge some blunders, take some shortcuts and keep the fire in your belly if the journey gets a bit tough.

Here's a recap to kick-start your journey:

Crafting your Road Map

Planning is the key to success for any small business. It acts as a road map, helping you wisely manage resources, set clear goals, and make informed decisions. Planning isn't about predicting every twist and turn; it's about being prepared for the unexpected and having a flexible framework to guide you.

Your North Star

Start by setting your compass to 'purpose'. Think about why you're on this journey in the first place. Your purpose is the anchor that will keep you grounded when storms arise, and the North Star that guides you when the path is unclear.

Navigating The Compliance Maze

Move through the compliance maze with caution. Stay compliant and understand the rules of the game. It might not be the most exciting part of the journey, but it ensures a smoother ride without unexpected obstacles and detours.

Stick to What You Are Good At

Many people get caught up in skilling up in every business area, leaving them stretched and tired, so play to your strengths. Just like a well-tuned instrument in an orchestra, each note you play should resonate with your core capabilities. This isn't the time to be a one-person band – it's about leveraging what you're good at and collaborating with others who complement your skills.

Master Your Money

Think of your finances as the fuel for your journey. Budget wisely. Have clear financial goals and keep personal and business finances separate. It's not about getting rich quick; it's about understanding the financial foundations to leverage and propel you forward.

Power to the People

Success isn't a solo expedition. Your team is your greatest asset. Nurture a positive work environment, surround yourself with talented individuals, and recognise the strength in collaboration with others. The people you take with you on the business bus can make the journey not only bearable but also enjoyable.

When Life throws you a Curve Ball

Expect the unexpected. Life tends to be full of twists and turns. Instead of swerving off course, learn to navigate them with finesse and embrace the changes. Adaptability, resilience and a 'can do' attitude is your secret weapon when facing unforeseen challenges.

Taking Care of Yourself

Amid the hustle, don't forget to pull over for self-care. Working 12 hours a day is not sustainable – neither for body nor for mind. Recharge, reflect, and ensure you have the stamina to face whatever lies ahead.

The Next Steps

Pearls of Wisdom

Along your route, you'll encounter pearls of wisdom. These are the insights gained from experience; the little nuggets that can save you from pitfalls. Cherish them. Learn from those who've travelled before you and let their wisdom guide your decisions.

My final tool to help you start your business is an easy-to-follow, step-by-step checklist that refers to the chapters in the book.

Start-up Checklist   EXAMPLE

Use this checklist to track your progress when you are starting your business.

Chapter	Topic	Completed
	Are you ready?	
1	Have you completed a SWOT Analysis?	YES/NO
1	Have you completed your Business Plan?	YES/NO
2	Have you completed your Mission Statement?	YES/NO
2	Have you drafted your Values?	YES/NO
2	Have you drafted your Vision Statement?	YES/NO
	Legal Obligations	
3	Have you sought advice on your business structure?	YES/NO
3	Do you know the tax implications for the structure you are using?	YES/NO
3	Have you registered an ABN?	YES/NO
3	Have you registered a business name?	YES/NO
3	Have you registered your trade mark?	YES/NO
3	Have you sought legal advice on your terms and conditions?	YES/NO
3	Have you applied for all relevant licences for your industry?	YES/NO
3	Have you researched or engaged with a broker on your insurance needs?	YES/NO
3 & 6	Do you know your legal obligations when employing staff?	YES/NO
	Advisors	
3 & 8	Do you have an Accountant?	YES/NO
3 & 8	Do you need a Bookkeeper?	YES/NO
3	Do you have an Insurance Broker?	YES/NO
3	Do you have a Lawyer?	YES/NO
8	Do you have a Mentor or Coach?	YES/NO
3 & 6	Do you have a Human Resources Advisor?	YES/NO
	Finances	
1 & 5	Can you afford to start a business?	YES/NO
5	Have you set up separate bank accounts?	YES/NO
5	Have you completed a budget?	YES/NO
5	Have you completed a cash flow forecast?	YES/NO
5 & 8	Do you have accounting software?	YES/NO
	Employing Staff	
6	Have you determined what staff you need?	YES/NO
6	Have you created a job description?	YES/NO

TOOLS

Chapter 1

- SWOT Analysis Tool
- One Page Business Plan

Chapter 2

- Mission Statement
- Business Values
- Vision Statement

Chapter 4

- Time Management Tool

Chapter 5

- Budget Template
- Cash Flow Forecast Template

Chapter 6

- Interview Questions

Chapter 8

- Nail that Goal Tool

What's Next

- Start Up Checklist

TO ACCESS THE FREE TOOLS, VISIT:
rise-above.au/
and use the password RISEABOVE

Glossary

ABN	Australian Business Number is a unique 11-digit number which is issued to all entities registered in the ABR.
ABR	Australian Business Register stores business and organisation details.
Accounts Payable	Outstanding payments the business currently owes to suppliers, vendors and creditors. Basically, it includes any bills you still need to pay.
Accounts Receivable	Outstanding payments all customers/ clients currently owe you.
ACN	Australian Company Number is a unique 9-digit number that every Company in Australia must have.
Adversity	Adversity refers to difficulties, challenges, or hardships that a person may face.
ASIC	The Australian Securities and Investments Commission is an independent Australian Government Body who regulates the conduct of Australian Companies, financial markets and financial services organisations.

Assets	An accounting category that represents anything a business owns; objects owned, or objects that have economic value to you.
ATO	Australian Taxation office is the Government's principal revenue collection agency.
Authenticity	The quality of being genuine or real.
BAS	The Business Activity Statement is a form submitted to the Australian Taxation Office by registered business entities to report their tax obligations, including goods and services tax, pay as you go withholding, pay as you go instalments, fringe benefits tax, wine equalisation tax and luxury car tax.
BAS Agent	Is a title protected by law and applies to an individual or entity who meets the requirement of the Tax Practitioners Board (TPB) for registration as an agent as specified in the Tax Agent Services Act (TASA) 2009.
Bookkeeper	Bookkeepers are responsible for providing accurate, up-to-date financial information about a business.
Budget	A spending plan based on income and expenses.
Business Plan	A documented strategy for a business that highlights its goals and its plans for achieving them.
Cash Flow	The net balance of cash moving in and out of a business at a specific point in time.
CPE	Continuing Professional Education is ongoing training that is required in order to remain certified as a professional.

Culture	The atmosphere, general customs and beliefs of a business.
Delegating	Transferring the responsibility for specific tasks from one person to another.
Entrepreneur	An individual who creates a new business.
Expenses	The money spent to obtain items necessary for your business.
Forecast	To calculate or predict.
GST	Goods and Services Tax a broad-based tax of 10% on most goods and services that are sold and consumed in Australia.
Income	The money you receive in exchange for a service or products.
Income Tax	The tax charged by the government on the annual income of an individual or business earned in a financial year.
Liabilities	Borrowed money that is yet to be repaid.
Mindset	The way our brain perceives ourselves and the world.
Multitasking	Attempting to perform multiple tasks at the same time.
Objectives	Specific goals and tasks you plan to achieve.
PAYG	Pay As You Go; an amount you take out of your employee's wages to cover tax is known as PAYG withholding.
Payroll Tax	A state or territory tax. It's calculated on the total wages you pay each month. The state or territory where your employees are located collects the tax. Not all businesses have to pay payroll tax.

Profitability	The ability of a business to earn a profit.
Resilience	The ability to bounce back after challenges and tough times.
Road Map	A visual way to connect strategy to actual work and deliver against goals.
Self-Assessments	The process of evaluating yourself, your skills, performance or ability.
Shareholders	A person, Company or institution that owns shares in a Company.
Sharepoint	A Microsoft web-based application that allows you to store and organise content and information.
Superannuation	A retirement planning scheme in which employers and employees contribute to a fund that provides income for the employee post retirement.
Sustainable	The ability to maintain or support a process continuously over time.
TFN	Tax File Number is a unique 9-digit personal reference number which identifies you in the tax and superannuation system.
Webinars	A seminar or presentation that takes place on the internet. People from different locations can attend; they can ask questions and answer polls.
Zoom™	A video conferencing platform that allows users to connect online for conference meetings, webinars and live chat.